Keeping Insects and Invertebra

C000116879

9.95

Frances Murphy

with illustrations by Denise Finney

John Bartholomew and Son Limited
Edinburgh

First published in Great Britain 1980 by
John Bartholomew & Son Limited,
12 Duncan Street, Edinburgh, EH9 1TA.

ISBN 0 7028 8020 5

1st Edition 1980
Reprinted 1983, 1985

British Library Cataloguing in Publication Data

Murphy, Frances
Keeping spiders, insects and other land invertebrates in
captivity—(Bartholomew pet series).
1. Invertebrates as pets
1. Title
639'.4   SF459.1/

Printed in Great Britain by
John Bartholomew & Son Limited

Contents

Introduction

The subjects of this book are drawn from a wide field and some are no more closely related to each other than they are to the reader. However, they are all small and consequently have a tendency to be classed together (very) loosely as 'insects'. One of their attractions (owing to their small size) is the possibility of keeping quite a substantial zoo in the sitting room. This book is principally written for those who wish to keep land invertebrates in the home as pets rather than in a laboratory.

Representatives of only two of the invertebrate phyla are discussed. Members of other phyla are confined to water or to a parasitic existence except for the earthworms. The giant earthworms are the largest of the terrestrial invertebrates. They can be 5-metres long and 7-cms in diameter. However, they cannot be kept in captivity and although ordinary English earthworms can be, and are, kept in captivity, they struck me as uninspiring pets.

The phyla considered are the Mollusca and the Arthropods. The largest invertebrate, the 15-metre long giant squid is a mollusc but the terrestrial representatives of the phylum, the slugs and snails, are all small. The Arthropods comprise the insects, the arachnids (spiders, scorpions, mites and their kin) millipedes, centipedes and crustacea (woodlice, prawns, crabs and so on) and one or two classes of rare and primitive creatures. This gives an enormous choice of possible subjects and I admit that my choice has been greatly influenced by a personal enthusiasm for the spiders and a general interest in the arachnids. Many possible insect pets have not been considered at all. All mention of the extremely successful beetles has been omitted. Not that they appear to be popular pets though some pest species are cultured in the laboratory. Less than justice has been done to the charming mantids.

Nearly all the pets and domestic animals kept by human beings are vertebrates. Few invertebrates have become domestic animals. Bees, although they have been kept since prehistoric times, are by no means truly domesticated and are still only too capable of taking off when swarming and setting up nests in hollow trees and living in the wild again. Beekeeping is undertaken for practical reasons and bees cannot be considered to be pets. Beekeeping is far too broad a subject for discussion here and there are many comprehensive books on bees and some excellent beekeeping societies which the aspiring beekeeper would be well advised to join.

Silkworms — the larval stage of the silkworm moth *Bombyx mori* —

have been kept in captivity so long that their habits and appearance have been considerably modified and it is not even completely certain from which species they are descended. Some people do keep them as pets and they are discussed in the chapter on caterpillars.

Flea circuses do not seem to be popular any more as they were in the thirties but anyone who wishes to keep pet fleas and set up a circus will find a fascinating (and totally off-putting) description in *'The Curiosities of Natural History'* 4th series by Francis Buckland (London, 1873).

Following this rather meagre history of invertebrate domestication, it is hardly surprising to find that the keeping of invertebrate pets is a recent innovation and that this book cannot therefore be based upon the centuries of experience that might assist in the writing of books on breeds of dogs or cats. All that this book can hope to offer is helpful suggestions, not hard and fast rules. The reader should watch his captives carefully and be prepared to modify his methods in the light of results, and to make cautious experiments. Most invertebrate pets will be kept out of interest rather than deep affection, but the sort of devotion that leads one to look at them every morning to see how they passed the night, ultimately pays off. These creatures do slowly respond by becoming less alarmed by and more tolerant of their owner. Probably this is partly the result of the owner's growing understanding of the animal, so one is well advised to go slowly with a new acquisition and not to attempt to make friends too quickly. It may sound ridiculous to talk slowly and soothingly to such pets. The justification for this behaviour is that it is difficult to make sudden, ill-considered movements while talking slowly.

Those who are keen on photography will find it a help to watch their subject for a time, considering the most desirable poses and how best to secure them, before getting the camera out. Photographers will find that invertebrates make very attractive and novel subjects and modern cameras, together with the handy and inexpensive little electronic flashes now available, make it reasonably (though not excessively) easy to obtain good results.

People who have no contacts in the biological world often have difficulties in obtaining equipment and acquiring the further knowledge they need. Most equipment has to be bought through the post from entomological dealers. The problem is to get the address of a suitable dealer. It will be a great help to join a local natural history society. Local libraries, museums and schools should have information about such societies. Dealers too may be able to give advice. Those who become enthusiastic about one particular group may want to join a national society which specialises in that group. If you write to a society to ask for information, please enclose a stamped and addressed envelope; you will probably not get an answer otherwise — most societies depend on subscriptions and though willing to help do not feel justified in spending their members' subscriptions paying what can be very heavy postage bills.

I have recommended a few books — mostly ones I have actually found helpful myself — but there are lots more. Do not despise children's books; they often have useful information. Public libraries, of course, are a mine of information. It may be a good idea to borrow a book you are considering buying to make quite sure that it really is the book you want.

For the purpose of exchanging information with other naturalists it is often essential to use scientific names. Many invertebrates do not have common names and even if they do, one name such as 'giant millipede' may refer to a large number of species. Even the scientific names are not completely free from confusion but they are more reliable than common names. One reason for the dislike of Latin names is uncertainty about their pronunciation. This is a quite unnecessary worry as there is no standard pronunciation and all sorts of variations are current.

I feel sure that the readers of this book would not wish to be a cause, however remote, of damage to the wild populations from which their captives are drawn. Therefore this book concentrates, as far as possible, on species which can be bred in captivity. It is also true that it is much more interesting to have pets which can be kept through the whole life cycle. On the other hand, it would be foolish to establish in one's home creatures which might become pests. The giant millipedes and land snails can do a good deal of damage in their native countries. They do even more if they are taken to other tropical countries and released. I can imagine the astonishment felt by tropical gardeners when they realise that people pay good money for their garden pests in temperate countries. However, pests, being tough, adaptable and philoprogenitive as they often are, can make very good pets. Tropical herbivores, like the millipedes and snails, are unlikely to become pests in a temperate climate, except possibly in a greenhouse — houses are too dry. On the other hand, many cockroaches can live on domestic scraps and could become a pest in a centrally heated house. Predatory invertebrates are unlikely to become pests even if they do become naturalised in houses.

Nothing has been said about disease. These creatures suffer from disease all right but too little is known about such matters to make it worth discussing the question.

Owners may wish to preserve their animals after death, either in the hope of getting unknown specimens identified or to build an interesting collection. Recommended methods of preservation differ according to type, and are described for each group. Roughly speaking specimens are either dried or immersed in 70 per cent alcohol. In Britain, industrial methylated spirits is the alcohol generally used and a permit for its purchase has to be obtained from the Customs and Excise Office.

I needed and was given a great deal of very generous help from fellow enthusiasts, who simply expressed the hope that their efforts would help others to share the pleasure and interest given by this hobby. I am particularly grateful to Bernard Betts, Henry Berman, Adam Cade, George Heath, Paul Hillyard, Judith Marshall, Philip Nussle, John Pontin, Adrian Rundle and Fred Wanless.

Food

It is highly desirable to consider the availability of food before acquiring any unusual pet. Suitable food is highly unlikely to be available in tins at local supermarkets and a reliable supply of food may take some time to organise. A slightly neglected garden will probably be a great help in solving this problem and in producing emergency supplies if the standard food runs short. Predatory or carnivorous invertebrates generally require live food of a convenient size and it is usually very difficult to persuade them to accept substitutes, such as small pieces of raw meat. A further problem with raw meat is its tendency to go off if not eaten immediately and it then becomes offensive. If live food is not eaten at once because the predator is not hungry this does not, in general, matter. However, if the predator is very old or about to moult and is confined with its intended prey in a rather small cage, the prey may fuss and upset the creature. Then the prey should be removed as soon as it is appreciated that it is not required and either released or fed to some hungrier animal. In the wild, predators presumably take a very wide range of prey. Fortunately, however, in captivity the needs of most predators can usually be satisfied by one or two standard cultures. *Drosophila* species, generally *D.melanogaster,* (the culture of which will be described later in the chapter) are the most useful of all live food for terrestrial invertebrate predators and, as they are widely used for genetic experiments, a good deal of effort has been given to establishing simple methods for culturing them and they are readily available. For many purposes wingless varieties are the most convenient, but it may be difficult to keep the culture uncontaminated by wild fully winged *D.melanogaster*. This fruit fly is by now found wild almost everywhere. Another useful food for predators is obtained by culturing ordinary domestic flies or by buying their larvae which are known as maggots or gentles. The latter term is common among fishermen who use these creatures as bait. Gentles can therefore often be bought from anglers' supply shops during the fishing season. The gentles will be taken by many invertebrate predators (provided they are large enough to tackle them) either as they are or when they have metamorphosed into flies. In this way a small quantity of gentles can serve as food for some time, particularly as their development can be slowed down by keeping them in a cool place, or speeded up by bringing them into a warm place. For the largest inverte-brate predators grasshoppers or locusts are a suitable food. Information on keeping these creatures will be found in the chapter on grasshoppers, as they make attractive pets in their own right as well as being a source of food. They are kept by many animal dealers as a food for reptiles and amphibians.

The herbivorous or vegetarian invertebrates present a different problem. For one thing they generally need to eat more, as vegetation provides less concentrated food than animal prey and so vegetarians eat more frequently and produce more excreta. Spiders, for example, need only to be fed once a week and if they are large and mature may only need to be fed once a month, or even less, while grasshoppers need fresh grass every day. Many herbivores accept only a limited range of plants. There is an interesting reason for this. Many plants incorporate poison in their tissues and these poisons protect them to a certain extent from the herbivores. There are several possible strategies to cope with this situation. Some herbivores reduce the quantity that they take from any one plant, nibbling a bit here and a bit there. This strategy is most convenient for larger creatures and is typical of that followed by rodents. Other creatures restrict themselves to a narrow range of plants to whose poison they are immune. Some even go so far as to incorporate the poison in their own tissues, becoming poisonous to predators as a result. The caterpillars of the Danaid or Monarch butterflies are a well-known example. They feed on milkweeds *(Asclepiads)* and incorporate the milkweed poisons in their tissues so that not only are they protected from predators, but they have even a host of imitators which gain some protection simply from looking like them! Some animals eat only non-poisonous plants, either specialising in one particular group like some caterpillars or eating a wide range of plants like most snails.

It is not at all easy to grow most plants indoors. The lack of light makes the plants weak and spindly and the atmosphere in the average home is too dry for any but special 'house plants'. In temperate climates grass and bramble *(Rubus fruticosus)* are available all the year round. Grass can, if necessary, be dug from under the snow. Bramble keeps well in water or wet sand if an inch of dry stem is cut off and the stem is placed in the water or wet sand immediately afterwards. Alternatively, the stem can be split or hammered to prepare it, just before it is placed in the water. Bramble is a suitable food plant for many stick insects and some caterpillars. Food plants should be examined before use to make sure that they do not harbour spiders or other predators. In Britain, for example, in the summer months, bramble frequently carries *Enoplognatha ovata,* a small white or red and white Theridiid that will take young stick insects a good deal larger than itself.

The problem of depleted food stocks due to winter conditions will be encountered mainly by keepers of exotic invertebrates. If local invertebrates are being kept in captivity, it can be assumed that they too could not find food at this season. The temperature should be reduced until the creatures become torpid and they should be left in peace and quiet until food is available. This technique can be cautiously applied to tropical creatures if no food is available. It is probably unsafe to drop the temperature of tropical invertebrates below 5°C (41°F) or of other invertebrates below freezing, 0°C (32°F). Although the temperature in many places falls well below freezing, there may be microhabitats which the animal can find where the temperature does not fall so low. It is best to be on the safe side and not subject a helpless captive to the most extreme conditions that it might have encountered in the wild. In times of scarcity it is not necessary to alter the temperature of the environment provided for snails. They react to low humidity by retiring into their shells and sealing their mouths with several layers of mucus, and can remain in this dormant state in a dry box for quite a time. *Achatina fulica* — the giant East African land snail, for instance, can probably last for a year under these circumstances and it is said that they used to be carried by native people on long journeys as a food supply. Around the shores of the Mediterranean during the hot months snails can be seen aestivating perched high in the air on walls, trees and plants.

Some invertebrates, such as giant land snails, can be fed on the discarded leaves from household vegetables or on over ripe fruit or apple cores, but most have specialised requirements.

Methods for growing particular food plants will vary widely with circumstances and advice as to how best to tackle the problem will be most easily and satisfactorily obtained locally from nurseries, horticultural societies and friends.

One of the most useful cultures for predatory invertebrates is, as has already been mentioned, the fruit fly *Drosophila melanogaster.* These flies feed on yeast and may be seen in warm weather investigating fermenting fruit. They are quite small, about 2-mm long, but can be produced in large quantities and several at a time fed, for example, to a spider. Spiders can look quite comic with their mouths full of fruit flies! Fruit flies can be cultured under suitable circumstances simply by leaving fermenting fruit in a container, but it is generally more convenient to use a standard medium.

Commercially produced dried preparations exist, such as Instant Drosophila Medium sold by T. Gerrard & Co. of Sussex (who also sell various breeding stock), which only need to be mixed with water and dried yeast to make up the medium. This should be done according to the directions given by the manufacturer. As an alternative there are various recipes for home production. It may be possible to make these recipes up in quantity and store them in a deep freeze. The author must admit to having avoided the trouble of making drosophila medium at home, relying entirely on the commercial product. However, here is a recipe:

> approx. 16-gms maize-meal or oat-meal
> approx. 1-gm agar
> approx. 8-gms brown sugar or black treacle

Add about 120-mls of water and boil for 15 mins. stirring well. Add a pinch 'Nipagin' or other mould deterrent and boil for 5 mins. While hot pour into 3-in x 1-in tubes to a depth of ¾-in or into half-pint bottles to a depth of 1½-in and add a pinch of dried yeast.

Alternatively, one can make up Instant Drosophila Medium in 3-in × 1-in tubes or in a half-pint bottle. The container used is a matter of choice. The most convenient arrangement depends on whether winged or wingless flies are being used. If wingless flies are being used and there is only a moderate need for flies, three 3-in × 1-in tubes produce a fair quantity of flies and they are easy to handle in the tubes which can be plugged with plastic foam. Alternatively, disposable plugs can be made of cotton wool balls wrapped in pieces of old nylon stocking. If mites have infected a culture it is better not to use the old plug again. When the plug is removed tapping the tube will be found to control the flies, which can

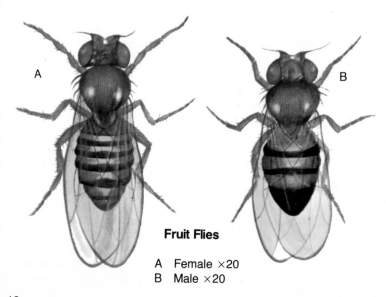

Fruit Flies

A   Female ×20
B   Male ×20

then be dropped into cages as required. Alternatively, they can be released into a bowl and caught again in small tubes which can then be used to introduce them into the cages. These methods do not work with winged flies. For them it is most convenient to have a container with a screw-on top. In the top is made a large hole about an inch in diameter and a small one about one-tenth of an inch in diameter. The larger hole, which is for ventilation, is plugged with plastic foam or some similar substance. The smaller is covered with a strip of sticky tape. When flies are required, the sticky tape is pulled back cautiously and a tube placed over the hole. The flies will walk up into it. Keep the tube mouth down and, using a piece of stiff paper if necessary, slide the tube onto its cork. The flies can then be transferred to wherever they are required. The author finds that winged fruit flies are only needed for feeding some web-making spiders. In general the wingless variety are much more useful, but there are circumstances in which it is difficult to keep the culture uncontaminated by wild winged flies. Contamination will cause flies to revert to the fully winged variety. The following has been found a satisfactory procedure. Keep the wingless culture in three 3-in x 1-in tubes as already mentioned. To begin with, three pairs of flies are put into each tube. It is fairly easy to distinguish the sexes although a magnifying glass will be needed. The tubes should be kept in a warm place, $20°-25°C$ $(68°-77°F)$ is the optimum. If the temperature falls too low, development will be very slow, and if the temperature is too high, the growth of mites, fungi and bacteria may become a nuisance. After a week or so the *Drosophila* larvae will crawl up the side of the tube and pupate. It is a good idea at this point to remove the breeding stock which may, of course, be used as food. If this is not done one may set up the next culture inadvertently using the elderly breeding stock which will not give as good results as using the young flies which have just emerged. When the new fruit flies emerge give them a few days to mate and to complete the main emergence, then set up a new culture using a pair of flies drawn from each old tube to stock each new tube so that in all nine pairs of flies form the new breeding stock. This appears to be sufficient to keep the culture going without degeneration for several years at least. The old cultures can be kept (preferably in a different room, since the old cultures are apt to get infested by mites which infect the breeding stock) till they cease producing more fruit flies. The author has found that keeping the tubes standing upright in a dish of water helps to prevent the cultures from drying out too rapidly. Everything should be kept as clean as possible. It is recommended that all the apparatus should be sterilized in a pressure cooker kept for this purpose. This is a council of perfection and whether one follows it depends on circumstances. If one is only keeping a small stock of flies, mite or other infestations are not so likely and if you can replace the flies easily then it does not matter so much anyway. It does seem sensible to use glass apparatus as it is easily kept clean. Scale — calcium carbonate which is deposited in hard water districts — can be removed by soaking the glass in dilute vinegar. The vinegar can be kept and used again.

The above procedures may sound tiresome but they can, of course, be adapted to suit individual circumstances and, if a number of predators are being kept, it is well worth-while having a reliable supply of food.

Also useful as food for predators are the larvae (known as maggots or gentles) of Calliphorids or flesh flies and the flies themselves. Gentles can be purchased at anglers' shops by those who live in areas where angling is popular. Alternatively, they can be cultured by exposing small pieces of meat. One of the most effective baits consists of the normally discarded intestines and other offal of a fowl. This is an insanitary procedure and results in an extremely unpleasant smell and must clearly be done out of doors. Chicken carcasses often carry Salmonella bacteria and strict personal hygiene should be observed when handling poultry. Further, as human views on what is or what is not edible are not necessarily the same as those of the rest of the animal kingdom, the bait must be protected or it will be carried off by cats or foxes. Fresh air round the bait is desirable in order to keep the smell under control. The following has been found to be a reasonable procedure. First take a plastic container, say 15-cm × 15-cm × 20-cm deep, preferably opaque with a lid, and put some sawdust in the bottom. The sawdust must be free of insecticide. Suitable sawdust should be obtainable at pet shops. Then take a clean empty tin about 10-cm or 12-cm high and put it in the container on the sawdust. On the top of the tin put the bait. Make a few holes in the sides of the container to enable the flies to reach the bait, and finally cover the box with some sort of rainproof lid and put a weight (half a brick, for example) on the lot in order to prevent cats from interfering with the gentle trap. Flies will lay eggs on the bait and the resulting larvae when they are fully fed will drop onto the sawdust, which will keep them comparatively clean. They can be removed and placed in a separate container, from which gentles can be taken as required until they pupate (after a length of time which will depend on the temperature). The pupae can be placed in cages and left to emerge in the predator's cage — some spiders will even eat pupae — or can be left to emerge in the container and then transferred to the cage. Gentles are a cheap and obviously nourishing food, but it must be admitted that the whole process is extremely insanitary and the necessity of washing and disinfecting hands and tools carefully after handling the gentle trap can be tiresome. However, treated in this way so that the bait becomes fairly dry, the gentle box should not be excessively smelly. Probably considerable

Gentle Box

A Sawdust   E Gauze for ventilation
B Bait   F Cover
C Lid of container G Weight
D Access holes   H Upturned tin

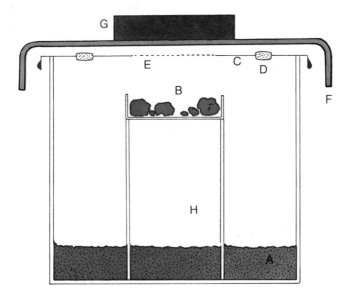

improvements could be made to the above apparatus by those who are good with their hands and have a feeling for design; the essential point being to keep the bait up in the air. Sometimes the gentle box attracts parasites such as ichneumons and chalcids in which case, unfortunately, many of the pupae will produce parasites instead of the desired flies. There is no obvious simple method of dealing with this problem. It may be possible to keep parasites out by plugging the entrance holes after a couple of days with plastic foam, which will allow some air in but keep out parasites. This depends upon the parasite being attracted by the presence of the fly larvae and not by the original bait, so that one can allow the flies to lay eggs and then shut out the parasites. Unfortunately chalcids are very small and hard to exclude. Some spiders will take the ichneumons but most spiders do not like them.

Further food can be collected in a sweep net or flies can be caught in various ways; snatched out of the air by the owners of good eyes, stalked with a tube by those with patience, or even caught in a butterfly net. Grubs and caterpillars which can be removed from garden produce may be popular with predators. In general it is often worth considering whether local pests will be enjoyed by your predators. Pest species are frequently those whose defence against predation is fast breeding rather than by being poisonous or aggressive. By definition there are lots of them, so that you will have identified a plentiful supply of food and your neighbours will not object to your feeding them to your pets as they might well do if, for example, rare and beautiful butterflies are being used as food.

Woodlice (sowbugs) are not widely eaten by predators, but for some spiders they seem to be preferred food, especially *Porcellio scaber.* They can generally be collected in quantity in damp places in the garden (or even in the house) and will stay alive for a long time in a plastic box, floored with slightly damp peat.

Mealworms *(Tenebrio molitor* or *T.obscurus)* feed on dry bran and are fairly easily cultured in a large opaque container covered with cloth and kept in a warm dark spot. They are popular food for vertebrate pets and are available from dealers. They do not seem to be very useful for feeding spiders, but further investigation would be worth-while.

Those who grow cabbages or any other *Brassica* will find that the cabbage whitefly *(Aleyrodes brassicae)* is useful food for very small spiderlings.

Large spiders will eat ordinary garden worms.

Termites are not found in Britain, but they are widespread in the tropics and sub-tropics. The workers provide food for lots of creatures. Although it is not possible to culture them they will survive for several days in a small closed tube with some damp vegetation and most species make useful food for suitably sized predators.

Springtails *(Collembola)* can be collected from amongst dead leaves or other litter by shaking low growing plants over a tray (sliding the tray under the plant, rather than attempting to take the plant to the tray) and by turning bricks. Sometimes they will collect on the surface of a shallow dish of water. They are accepted by such predators (small wolf spiders for example) as are able to capture them, but their ability to escape by making terrific leaps into the air limits their usefulness.

Cages and other Equipment

Few cages are manufactured for the purpose of keeping land invertebrates and the reader will generally have to make his or her own, or use, with or without adaptation, apparatus which has been produced for some quite different purpose. Suggestions are also made in this chapter concerning tools and equipment which may be found useful.

Aquariums, whether glass or plastic, make useful cages. Plastic aquariums are lighter and consequently easier to handle, cheaper and less breakable and are the best choice if you intend to buy an aquarium. Glass aquariums, which do not need to be watertight, are useful and can often be acquired cheaply. The cage can be finished with netting or even a piece of material, held on with elastic. Black netting is easier to see through than white and is preferable for this purpose, but it is not easy to come by. It may be found at a drapers shop because it is mainly used for decorating hats. The most useful size of aquarium for insects is about 30-cm × 20-cm × 20-cm. The author employs a double loop of string into which a strong elastic band is fitted to hold the net cover in place. This sort of cage can be used for keeping many araneamorph spiders, mantids, phasmids and orthoptera. Food can be introduced by lifting a corner of the netting. For feeding spiders it may be more convenient to make a hole in the net. A small cross is cut in the net and a cork worked into the hole. Then if the food has been captured in a tube of the same size as the cork, the cork can be removed and the tube emptied through the hole in the net.

Propagators, which are available at seed merchants and garden shops, can also be utilized as useful cages. For stronger inmates, such as giant land snails and tarantulas, it may be desirable to tie the lid and the tray together. For some pets there may be insufficient ventilation and panels of net may need to be let into the sides of the propagator cover.

Many household objects, such as sandwich boxes, cake tins, tumblers and convenience food containers are made of clear plastic and are useful for small insects. It may be desirable to bore a few holes in the lid, but since none of these containers is completely airtight, and most invertebrates do not need a lot of oxygen, this may not be necessary. The plastic cylinders in which some goods are packed can also make good cages.

Some engineering parts come in small plastic boxes which make excellent cages for small spiders and phasmid eggs. Entomological dealers sell plastic 'pill boxes' which are round with push-on lids 2.5-cm high and 5-cm in diameter. These are also useful for small spiders and phasmid eggs.

Jam jars, especially the larger ones, are useful. The original tops usually become rusty rather soon but they can be replaced by netting tops.

For some spiders cardboard boxes, such as shoe boxes or shirt boxes, are useful. Panels can be cut out and netting or cellophane (according to what is needed) sewn or fastened with sellotape in their place.

For many of the lighter insects and spiders, cages made entirely of netting fastened round a framework of metal, meccano for example, or wood is satisfactory. Some thought must be given to introducing food and in due course extracting the occupant. A zip can be inserted in the netting or it can just be unsewn, food being inserted through a corked hole as already described.

Satisfactory upright cylindrical cages for caterpillars, phasmids and mantids can be made from acrylic sheet. A rectangular piece is bent round into a cylinder and fitted top and bottom into two large lids (of the same size). The seam can be fastened with sellotape, or a more satis-factory seam could be made by punching a series of holes along both edges (about 2.5-cm apart) with a small leather punch, and 'sewing' the seam together with strong cotton or thin string. There are, of course, many possible variations on this theme.

Cylindrical cages for rearing caterpillars (also suitable for mantids and stick insects) can be bought from entomological dealers.

Good carpenters can make cages of wood and glass or plastic sheet with perforated zinc panels for ventilation. These will be better looking than the cheaper and more rapidly made cages discussed above. On the whole, metal is best avoided for cages because of its tendency to rust in the damp conditions it would be subjected to.

Corked glass or plastic tubes are sometimes used as cages, particu-larly for small spiders, but their tendency to roll about, upsetting their inhabitants, makes them inconvenient as cages. However, a few tubes about 1-cm in diameter are very useful for catching and handling live food. They can be bought from entomological dealers.

Forceps or tweezers are useful for moving things about. They can be bought from entomological dealers, stamp dealers and sometimes watch menders might get you a pair if you cannot find them elsewhere. Eyebrow tweezers — not so convenient, but cheaper, — can be found at the chemist. Scissors are endlessly useful and will be readily available.

Magnifying glasses are essential for those keeping really small creatures and they add greatly to the interest of keeping even the larger

Plastic aquarium topped with netting

Large plastic container

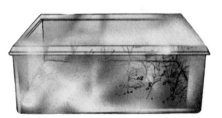

'Lunch Box'

Small plastic containers

Various Cages

Facing page:

A 'Wet Box'
B Thermometer
C House-plant spray
D Instrument for measuring humidity
E Watchmaker's loop ×8
F House-plant (Bryophyllum tubiflorum)
G Eye dropper
H Watchmaker's loop for attaching to spectacles
J Low power magnifying glass ×2
K Storksbill tweezers
L Tweezers
M Corked tubes
N Pencil
O Labels
P Small bag of sand

---

invertebrates. Ideally one needs a low power magnifying glass, X2 or X3, with a field of view at least 5-cm across and a higher power up to 10X. These can be bought at some opticians, stamp dealers, or entomological dealers. For anyone keeping small spiders a watchmaker's loop (or for spectacle wearers a small magnifier that can be fastened onto the spectacle frame) will enable you to feed and care for small spiders much more easily. The author has found the latter device absolutely invaluable, although initially quite difficult to obtain.

Watering devices of various kinds are useful. An eye dropper can be bought from the chemist and used to deliver a single drop of drinking water onto the side of a cage. It can also be used to drip water onto the netting top of a cage so that water sprinkles the whole cage. Small house-plant or greenhouse sprays are useful for spraying the food plants of phasmids, thus providing humidity.

It is useful to have a small device for measuring humidity either in the room or in a heated cage if one is provided. These are not easy to find but can be purchased from suppliers of greenhouse equipment or bought from scientific equipment manufacturers.

It is sometimes useful to grow a small plant in a cage, for example, as a mould-free support for small webs in a humid cage, or to prevent soil from becoming too damp. The environmental conditions in a cage — poor light, overheating, etc. — are too fierce for most plants and few house-plants are likely to be able to endure them. The toughest and most useful the author has come across is *Bryophyllum tubiflorum*. It is not one of the most ornamental plants, but it can be maltreated without fatal results. Small plantlets drop from the ends of the tubular leaves and grow up without attention, and cuttings can be placed into wet sand or soil, where they will often root and grow. A supply can be kept without trouble, except for occasional watering. Sand and peat, but particularly sand, are often

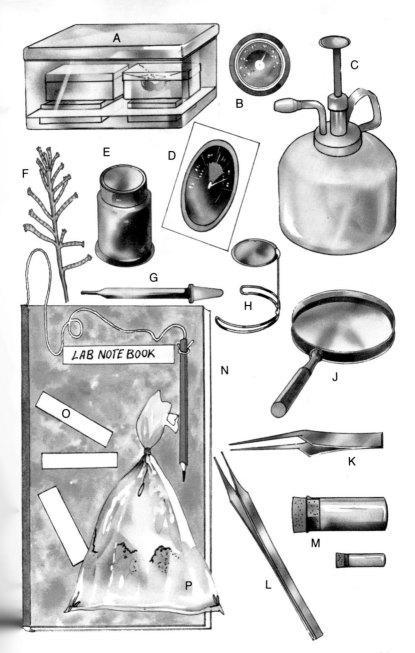

LAB NOTE BOOK

useful for flooring cages, but where plants are to be grown, a sterilized potting compost could be used.

A thermometer is extremely useful. Ideally, you should have a heated cabinet with a thermostat but this is expensive and hardly seems necessary unless you are keeping exotic and expensive insects. It is much simpler to measure the actual temperature in your home and, if it is not sufficient, to supply extra heat.

It may be desirable to establish a hot box by placing a heater in an old aquarium. If the aquarium is large and fitted with a reasonably air-tight lid, a low output heater, such as those used in seed trays, or a 60-watt bulb, will cause the temperature to rise by about 6°C (10°F). Such an arrangement will provide room for several small cages. It is generally the younger (and hence smaller) stages of tropical invertebrates that most need heat. The seed tray heater is preferable to the 60-watt bulb as it will operate for a long time with no maintenance. Heater pads are advertised by some pet shops and possibly they too will operate for long periods without attention.

Some small invertebrates — particularly spiders — need a good deal of humidity and since cages in the hot box tend to dry out very quickly, care needs to be taken to provide the humidity required. To overcome this problem a small 'wet box' can be used to humidify the hot box. A plastic box with a few holes in the lid is partly filled with water and the cages are then placed on blocks just clear of the water. This keeps a satisfactory humidity in the smaller cages. If a slightly more humid environment is required, the small cages can have a floor of paper towel which has been flattened with a couple of drops of water. The paper towel will get nasty and need to be replaced every few weeks. For creatures that really need a very humid atmosphere, sphagnum moss holds a good deal of water and does not get mouldy, but it needs light and must be watered with lime-free water. In these circumstances, sphagnum in a more or less air-tight cage will keep going for a long time and needs no soil. It provides a satisfactory environment for marsh and bog-loving creatures.

ON NO ACCOUNT must glass or plastic cages be placed in direct sunlight, as the resulting rise in temperature (owing to the greenhouse effect) may easily be sufficient to kill the inhabitants.

Finally, anyone who is keeping a number of invertebrates will find it well worth-while to have strong paper, pencil and scissors nearby for making labels, which can be placed in the cage or sellotaped neatly to the outside of the cage. A notebook for interesting observations and for recording treatment of your pets (so that successful treatment can be repeated and other treatments abandoned) will be found useful. It is so easy to forget exactly what occurred!

Arthropods

All the creatures considered in this book, with the exception of the snails (Mollusca), belong to the Arthropods. This enormous Phylum contains three quarters of all the known animals and their way of life includes predators, vegetarians, detritus (or rubbish) eaters and parasites. They are found everywhere, on land and in the sea.

Their body plan has one major limitation. Although there exist monstrous crabs with a leg span of 3.5-metres, in general they are all small, and a land invertebrate with any dimension approaching 30-cm is exceptional.

The skin of an arthropod is usually heavily armoured and rigid and there is no internal skeleton, but instead the rigid skin forms an 'exoskeleton'. This prevents movement except at the joints and even there movement is usually more constrained than it is in a vertebrate limb. Arthropods tend to have more joints to a limb than is the case with vertebrates. The advantages that this coat of armour provides in the way of protection from predators and from the other great enemy, dehydration, are obvious. Equally obvious is the problem of growth. All arthropods have to shed their skins a number of times (somewhere between five and twelve times on average) during their growing period. Moulting or ecdysis is very dangerous for the animal and accounts for much of the mortality among invertebrate pets. Many, but not all, moult by hanging themselves up and using gravity to help extract them from their old skin. The new exoskeleton forms beneath the old and a lubricant is produced which helps in moulting — in fact one suspects that insufficiency of this lubricant may account for a number of moulting failures. Too dry an atmosphere can also account for some failures, but excessive dampness can be disastrous to arthropods which like it hot and dry. In general it is unwise to interfere with or move an arthropod in the middle of a moult.

Frequently a limb is lost in the process of moulting or one which has formed badly is removed by the animal. This is a process known as automism which is a voluntary casting off of a limb often as a defence against a predator. The limb breaks off at a predetermined spot and the area heals with little or no loss of fluid. The lost limbs normally regenerate at the next moult — provided that there is another moult. The new limb may be rather thin, but after the following moult it will usually be back to normal. As far as possible arthropods should not be handled because of this tendency to cast limbs, and they should never be picked up by one leg.

Facing page:

A	Crustaceans	K	Hymenoptera
B	Millipedes	L	Diptera
C	Centipedes	M	Scorpions
D	Incomplete metamorphosis	N	Uropygids
E	Phasmids	O	Amblypygids
F	Mantids	P	Spiders
G	Orthoptera	Q	Pseudoscorpions
H	Complete metamorphosis	R	Solifuges
J	Lepidoptera	S	Harvestmen

Invertebrates, including arthropods, lack means of internal control of their temperature. This obviates the necessity of the quantities of food that vertebrates need and enables them to do with much less oxygen also, but it means that in cold weather they become torpid and do not eat or grow. Some arthropods are adapted to operate at very low temperatures, living for instance under the Arctic snow, but tropical pets must be kept warm if they are to do well. It is quite noticeable that tropical arthropods can be much faster moving than those from temperate countries.

The family tree shows a rough idea of the relationships of the arthropods discussed in this book. Many of the component groups contain thousands of species. These groups are studied by specialists who tend to develop their own terms for such things as parts of the body, life phases and so on, so that the terms used tend to vary from order to order in a way that can be confusing to the non-specialist.

The main classes in which we are interested are the crustaceans (mostly marine), the millipedes and centipedes, the insects, and the arachnids.

The woodlouse or sowbug is the only crustacean mentioned in this book and then only as possible food. They are rather vulnerable both to dehydration and to drowning, but they seem to cope competently with moulting. They moult one half of the cuticle or skin at a time and rarely seem to have trouble.

The millipedes and centipedes form two different classes, the millipedes being vegetarian, or at any rate non-predatory, and the centipedes being predators. Both are vulnerable to dehydration. The millipedes moult their cuticles in a series of rings. The keeping of large tropical millipedes and centipedes is a very new venture and there is not a lot of reliable information available.

Arthropods

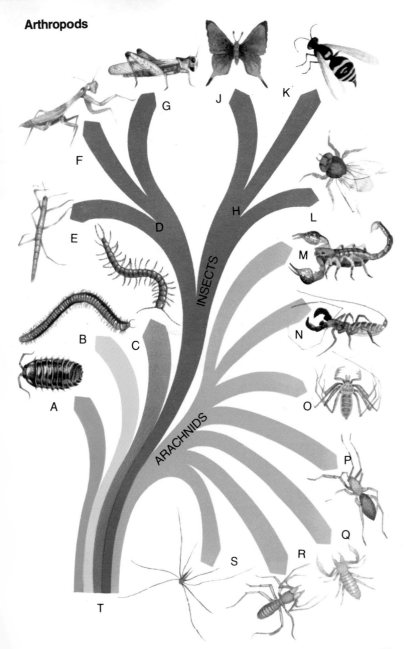

The insects are the largest class of arthropods. Some of them have developed very effective defences against dehydration — some of the Orthoptera, for example, only thrive in dry conditions. Most insects are winged as adults, but the immature stages do not have wings. The young of most arthropods — as indeed of most animals — more or less resemble their parents, often with different proportions, and grow more like them with each successive moult, finally developing sexual organs and in the case of many insects, wings. However, in the most highly evolved orders of insects the egg hatches into a worm-like larva which in the case of the Lepidoptera is known as a caterpillar. The larva is well-adapted as a food gathering creature and when it is fully fed it hides away and becomes a pupa, a dormant stage during which it undergoes a remarkable metamorphosis, finally moulting into the imago or adult insect which, in the case of the Lepidoptera, is called a butterfly or moth. The larvae of flies are known as maggots or, in the case of those suitable as fishing bait, gentles. The larvae of ants (also bees and wasps) are helpless, seldom seen creatures which are tended in the nest by adult insects. The young stages of insects which do not undergo a complete metamorphosis are known as 'nymphs' or in the case of grasshoppers sometimes as 'hoppers'.

The final class is the Arachnida — spiders, scorpions, harvestmen, mites, solifuges and others. Most of these orders are predatory — many of the mites being exceptions. Some of them are adapted for life in deserts, the scorpions particularly having many species which like hot, dry places.

Caterpillars or Lepidoptera

Caterpillars are the food gathering and growing stage of the lepidoptera or butterflies and moths. These insects go through four distinct phases. The perfect insect or imago — called a butterfly or moth as the case may be — lays eggs or ova, from which hatches the caterpillar or larva. When the caterpillar is fully grown (after a number of moults and a considerable increase in size) it moults into a chrysalis or pupa. During this apparently quiescent stage the body is entirely reformed and finally the perfect insect emerges to mate and lay eggs. There are about 120,000 lepidoptera in the world and although they are the most popular of the insect orders, there is still a great deal to learn about them.

The first problem for the would-be keeper of caterpillars is discovering the right food plant and ensuring an adequate supply of it. Caterpillars are fussy about what they will eat, and caged up with unsuitable food will make no effort to eat it but will wander about in a hopeless search for the right food until they die. If eggs or caterpillars are taken from the wild, it may be assumed that they will have been found on the correct food plant. The lepidopterist must be prepared to take quite an interest in botany and learn to recognise plants from their leaves alone, when necessary.

The eggs are kept in small plastic boxes or glass topped tins. They do not need any more air than will get to them in these circumstances. The temperature at which they are kept will depend upon the type of lepidoptera in question. Native species being over-wintered should be kept in a dry but unheated outhouse to prevent them getting dessicated or emerging early before their plant food has started into growth. Exotic species may need special treatment. The eggs should be examined daily; generally speaking they will darken shortly before hatching. Many caterpillars make their first meal by eating the discarded egg-shell and they must not be prevented from doing this. It is probably best to leave them to begin with in the plastic box in which the eggs were kept. A small quantity of fresh tender food plant should be introduced into the box very shortly before or just after hatching. It should be renewed frequently, every day or two, to begin with and the frass (as caterpillar droppings are called) removed. All this must be done carefully without any rough handling of the caterpillar, as far as possible without handling it at all. The old food plant can be removed with forceps or tweezers and the part on which the caterpillars are resting snipped off and returned to the cage.

The food plant should be dry, not damp with rain, dew or melted frost. It should not be covered with honeydew — that sugary substance produced by aphids which sometimes covers leaves — and if it is, the honeydew must be washed off carefully and the leaves allowed to dry before the food plant is offered to the caterpillar. Some caterpillars are apt to drown in any water that is available to them; even drops of condensation on the side of the cage can be fatal. Small pieces of absorbent paper may be useful in preventing condensation.

As they grow, they will need to be moved to larger cages. It is generally considered that larger plastic boxes, such as 'lunch' boxes, make good cages. No holes need be bored in the lid. Some air enters when the food plant is renewed and caterpillars do not need a great deal. Also the food plant keeps better under these conditions. If the food plant is actually growing in a pot it may be more convenient to put the caterpillars onto the growing plant and put the whole lot into a convenient cage. It would be best to have a certain amount of ventilation in this case, as transpiration from the plant may otherwise cause condensation. If the food plant is kept in a vase of water, great care must be taken to prevent the caterpillar from walking down the food plant (a natural thing for it to do when seeking access to a fresh bit of food plant) and drowning itself. However, if a prized caterpillar is found with its head down in the water it may yet be possible to save it. Place it on a piece of blotting-paper and warm it on a radiator, by a fire, or even very cautiously over a flame. Caterpillars moult several times, during which operation they must not be moved. Before a moult they will cease feeding for a bit and may seem rather unwell. If the required food plant is a tree or bush growing in the garden, one can 'sleeve' the caterpillars, placing them on the tree in a muslin sleeve, which is placed round the branch and tied tightly at both ends. If it is not tied tightly, earwigs will get in and cause damage. Although caterpillars are plant feeders, they can become cannibal, both killing and eating other members of their own species; this being most likely in conditions of overcrowding and near starvation.

In due course the caterpillar will come to pupation. If exotic lepidoptera are being kept, it should be known to which species they belong. Even if they are native species they have with any luck been identified. This is desirable because various species differ widely in their choice of sites for pupation. Some pupate on the food plant, either in the open fastened to a leaf or twig, or in a cocoon built among the leaves. Others prefer to descend the plant and pupate among the herbage at the base of the food plant or even under the soil; yet others use cracks in bark or similar spots. If the caterpillar is of an unknown species, all these possibilities must be provided for.

When the caterpillar demonstrates by its restless wanderings its readiness for pupation, it should be removed to a pupation cage provided with a sprig of food plant, a piece of bark, or some soil substitute such as bulb fibre (ordinary soil is not really suitable in these artificial circumstances), or all three in the case of an unknown species. The pupa can then be left until it emerges. If it is moved, it must at least be left untouched for a week, if not longer. A close watch must be kept for mould, especially near the pupa, as this can spread on a pupa and effectively stifle it.

When the butterfly or moth finally emerges it will need some twigs on which to perch while its wings dry off and harden. If you wish to kill the imago in order to have a perfect specimen, this should not be done until the wings have dried and hardened.

Female lepidoptera can usually be distinguished from males by their much stouter abdomens, resulting from the eggs which are already present there. The abdomen of the male has a pair of claspers at the end, but these are not always easy to see, particularly in the case of butterflies. Of course, in many species the sexes can easily be separated by the shape or pattern of the wings.

Nymphalis Io

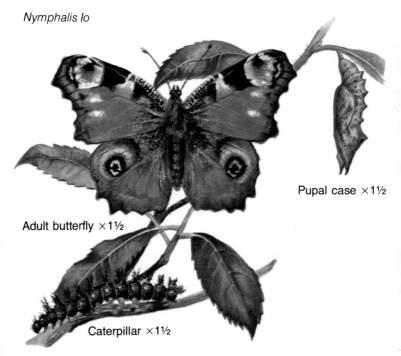

Pupal case ×1½

Adult butterfly ×1½

Caterpillar ×1½

Bombyx mori — the silkworm — is the only truly domesticated inverte-brate. It is not even certain from which ancestral species it has been developed. Its behaviour has been much modified and it could not survive in the wild any more, unlike the hive bee which has been little modified by its long association with man, and is still essentially a wild creature. The silkworm, besides being reasonably easy to keep, is an interesting creature. Its food plant is the mulberry, preferably the white mulberry *(Morus alba)*. The common mulberry usually found in gardens is the black mulberry *(Morus nigra)*. This has a delicious black fruit (vaguely like a blackberry); the white mulberry has a white fruit which darkens slightly when ripe. To provide a constant source of food for silk-worms, it is necessary to have a mulberry tree available. Eggs are laid in August or September and can be kept in a cool, dry place until mid-May when mulberry leaves (mulberry is deciduous) become available. The eggs can then be brought into the warm to hatch. It is usual to rear the silkworms in trays and supply them with enough food to reduce the tendency to wander. They should be given fresh food morning and evening (their feeding times) and stale leaves removed. Their surround-ings must be kept clean.

In order to obtain nice clean silk cocoons it is recommended that the silkworms are confined in paper cones for pupation. They need warmth at this time. After about ten days the silk can be removed without killing the creature. Loose silk is removed and the cocoon soaked in warm water. Then the silk can be loosened and most of it wound off. During emergence the moth spoils the silk so that afterwards it is useless. There is no difficulty in getting the adults to pair.

The silk moths or *Saturniidae* are popular and beautiful lepidoptera. There is one British representative of this family, but most of them are tropical in origin. They will however feed on European fruit trees, privet, oak, hawthorn and other reasonably available food plants though, of course, different species do not all eat the same substitute plant. Pairing may be difficult to ensure as depending on the species different conditions are needed. However, if large beautiful exotic moths are desired, silk moths are obviously worth trying. The Amateur Entomolo-gical Society has produced a useful handbook on the subject.

This large and popular group of invertebrates has only been discussed very briefly. This is because there is a wealth of good books on the subject. A random selection is given below. You can also join an entomo-logical society, most of which welcome serious beginners, or a local natural history society, which will often have one or two members who are lepidopterists. In these societies there should be plenty of help and free advice available.

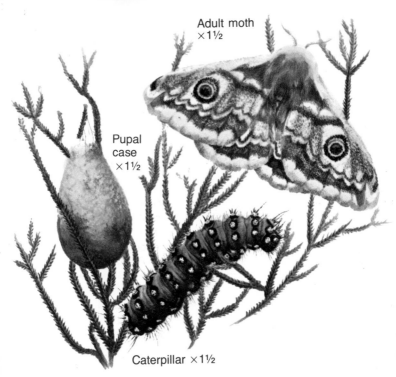

Adult moth ×1½

Pupal case ×1½

Caterpillar ×1½

Saturnia pavonia (Emperor moth)

Books

Your Book of Butterflies and Moths — H.B.D. Kettlewell (Faber & Faber 1963)
The Butterflies of the British Isles — R. South (Warne)
The Moths of the British Isles — R. South (Warne)
The Caterpillars of the British Butterflies — W.J. Stokoe (Warne)
The Caterpillars of the British Moths — W.J. Stokoe (Warne)
Studying Insects — R.L.E. Ford (Warne, 1973)
Butterflies and Moths, A guide to the more common American Species — R.T. Mitchell and H.S. Zim (Golden Press, New York)
Silkworm Rearing — B.A. Cooper (A.E.S. Leaflet No. 3)
A Silkmoth Rearer's Handbook — W.J. Crotch (A.E.S.)

A.E.S. Publications available from: A.E.S. Publications Agent, 129 Franciscan Road, Tooting, London, SW17 8DZ, England.

Ants

Ants belong to the Hymenoptera, along with wasps, bees and various other insects. They are a large family with 3,500 described species, about 46 of which are found in Britain. Some of the British species are parasitic in the nests of other species. Ants belong to an order which undergoes a full metamorphosis. Ant larvae are particularly helpless and are cared for by the workers — sterile females that freed from egg laying are able to run the nest, caring for the larvae, cleaning the nest, guarding it and finding and bringing home food. The pupae are also cared for by the workers. At certain seasons 'alates' or winged males and females, whose function is to mate, are produced. After mating the males do not last long but the females after finding a possible new nest site — or returning to their old one — shed their wings and start life in the nest. Some very small ants will fly and mate in a large sandwich box, but in general it is not practical to arrange this. So keeping ants presents quite different problems from those involved in keeping the other creatures in this book. For one thing a colony of ants — it might better be described as a large family — is kept rather than an individual or a number of individuals. A colony has an indefinite life span and can in fact be expected to last five years at least and maybe fifteen or twenty. Exotic ants are not imported — except inadvertently — and ant colonies from the garden can be brought into the house for study. They can then be released again if so desired.

Artificial ant nests are known as 'formicaria' and plaster of Paris nests can be purchased from entomological dealers. Essentially they consist of a nest area which is enclosed, possibly darkened and kept damp, and a feeding area which is kept dry and where food is given. The main problems are keeping the nest area damp and preventing the ants from escaping. To consider the latter problem first, one solution is to stand the formicarium on legs which have been placed in small pots of water, oil or some repellent fluid, but this is messy and in due course the ants can walk over the film of dust and dead ants which collects on it. Large ants — such as wood ants *(Formica rufa)* — can be prevented from walking up a vertical surface by painting it with polytetrafluoroethylene (Fluoron), but small ants manage to walk up this in time. The best solution is to keep the ants totally enclosed.

With plaster of Paris nests there is no difficulty in keeping the nest area damp as the plaster absorbs water but, as a result, it goes mouldy and then mites arrive and they can cause considerable damage to the ants.

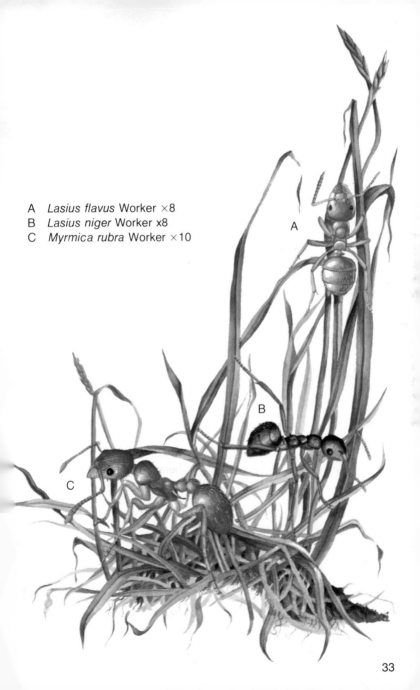

A *Lasius flavus* Worker ×8
B *Lasius niger* Worker x8
C *Myrmica rubra* Worker ×10

33

Ants nest, under construction

A Wick
B Concrete
C Nest chamber
D Glass
E Exit tube
F Plasticine
G Foraging area
H Reservoir of water

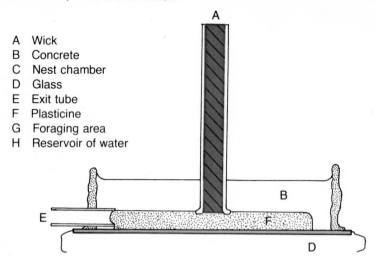

Completed nest

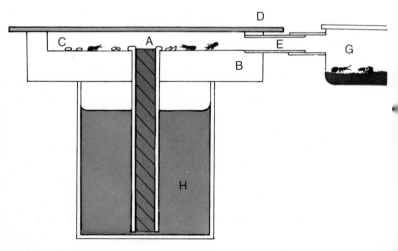

Even if one succeeds in preventing moulds, a plaster of Paris nest is not as long-lived as the ant colony will very likely prove to be. Consequently, a more satisfactory result will be obtained by casting the formicarium in concrete. Packets of cement and sand ready mixed for making concrete can be bought from Do-It-Yourself shops. A wick should be provided which can be immersed in a reservoir of water. If the ants have a supply of water they can, if necessary, be neglected for several weeks and still survive. An exit tube which can be connected to the feeding area which could be a closed lunch box with a suitable hole for the tube. The best material so far found for the wick is a suitably sized piece of fire brick. This is rather brittle stuff but otherwise works very well and keeps clean. Failing that, a tube full of plaster of Paris is the next best thing. The nest chamber should be about 1-cm deep for small and ordinary sized ants, i.e. the common garden ant *Lasius niger* and smaller ants. It should be larger for *Formica rufa,* the wood ant, but it would be more sensible to start keeping ordinary garden ants. Wood ants present a number of problems.

As shown in the diagrams, a piece of glass will be needed and if the instructions are followed carefully it will fit smoothly over the top of the nest, but will admit enough air to provide the necessary ventilation. A thin piece of wet tissue paper is squeegeed onto the glass plate to prevent the cement sticking to the glass. Then a wall of plasticine (or modelling clay) is made to fix the boundaries of the nest. A nest chamber is made of plasticine and the exit tube laid in place through the boundary wall and abutting onto the nest chamber. Finally, the wick is held in place as shown. The concrete is then poured in and the whole thing left for a week to set. After a week the plasticine is carefuly scraped out and the nest is ready to use. The nest area need only be five or ten square centimetres in size. If no earth is provided in the feeding area it is not necessary to darken the nest, but if earth is available the ants will use it so cover the glass. However, it is easy enough to lay a piece of black paper on the glass and probably better for the ants.

Ants do not need an enormous amount of food. A few drops of sugar solution every few days and some freshly killed insects, such as fruit flies or domestic flies, will provide them with both carbohydrate and protein.

Other designs of nests are described in *'Ants'* by M.V. Brian, and still further designs using the ever present plastic boxes could be tried.

Red ants *(Myrmica species),* black garden ants *(Lasius niger)* and yellow ants *(Lasius flavus)* are common in gardens and probably would be the most sensible ants to start with. *Myrmica* species are best of all, because although they sting, there are several queens to a nest, and a queen is needed to form a proper colony. The queens are noticeably larger than the workers but, although the queens and the males have wings when they are first hatched and when they leave the nest to mate, the queens remove their wings before starting a colony or returning to their original colony.

For those who find ants difficult to handle, one recommended method is to drop them into a bowl of cold water, into which a drop of domestic detergent has been introduced to reduce the surface tension. The ants will sink to the bottom and the wanted ants — say ten workers and a queen — can be sorted out. Strain them off with a tea strainer and put them in the nest. They will soon recover and settle in. Ants are very tough and can survive quite a long immersion.

One of the interesting things about ants is the variety of creatures that live in their nests with them. There is the small white woodlouse *(Platyarthrus hoffmannseggi),* a number of spiders, beetles and a host of other insects. It is fascinating to watch the interaction of these creatures. It is also, of course, interesting to watch the normal life of the nest, care of the young larvae, and so on.

Ants can be preserved dry, or in 70 per cent alcohol.

Books

Ants — M.V. Brian (Collins 1977)
The Ant World — D.W. Morley (Penguin Books, 1953)
British Ants — H.St.J.K. Donisthorpe (Routledge, 1927)
The Insect Societies — E.O. Wilson (Belknap Press of Harvard University Press, Cambridge, Massachusetts, U.S.A.)

Mantids

The mantids are a family of about 1,800 carnivorous insects. They belong to a primitive insect group and do not have a complete metamorphosis; that is to say they hatch out of the egg looking much like their parents, and after a variable number of moults (from three to twelve) become adult. They develop wings only in the final moult like other winged insects.

All mantids are carnivorous and catch their prey by perching in some suitable spot and waiting for the arrival of a suitable insect, when they lash out with their heavily armoured first pair of legs. These legs shut like a trap on the victim, which is then held up and eaten from side to side, for all the world like someone eating corn on the cob. They are generally beautifully camouflaged in their natural surroundings. *Phyllocrania paradoxa* from East Africa, for example, imitates a dead leaf so accurately that even when a specimen was held up on a dead twig for visitors to admire, most people were unable to see her.

Mantids lay their eggs in oothecae, curious constructions in which egg chambers have been surrounded by hardened foam and the whole enclosed by a tough outer layer. This is deposited on twigs, bark, under stones, or on walls and such-like places. The oothecae differ in appearance according to type, and with experience one will know what sort of mantid to expect from a given ootheca. These oothecae can sometimes be bought from dealers and are advertised, for example, in *'Exchange & Mart'*.

Mantids are mainly creatures of warm and humid places, such as tropical rain forests, but they are found in Europe as far north as Paris, and in America they reach as far as New York. They are also found in deserts or near desert areas though one suspects that they have means of keeping to microhabitats where they are somewhat protected from dessication.

It is worth taking a good deal of trouble to discover exactly where your ootheca came from, but it is probably safe to assume that the early stages, at least, require warmth and humidity.

In spite of the efforts that mantids make to protect their young, oothecae are frequently infested with parasitic types of small wasps. These wasps can also be very interesting and it would be worth making enquiries among your entomological friends to find out if anyone would be pleased to have them.

Facing page:
A *Stagmomantis limbata* Female ×⅔
B *Pseudocreobotra wahlbergi* Female ×1
C *Polyspilota aeruginosa* Female ×1
D *Tenodera superstitiosa* Nymph ×⅔
E *Phyllocrania paradoxa* Female ×2
F Ootheca ×1
G Ootheca ×1

The ootheca should be attached to a twig or something similar and placed in the breeding cage. The latter should be kept warm and slightly humid with an occasional light spray. A temperature in the range of 21–26°C (70–79°F) is most suitable. A good sized breeding cage with growing plants established is best of all. For the sake of the plants it must be in a well-lit place but out of direct sunlight. The young mantids hatch in two to six months, depending on type and circumstances. Anything from 20–300 young may be expected and though they generally emerge quickly it may take several weeks for the emergence to be completed. They let themselves down on a fine thread, on which they hang while they dry off and their skins harden. Then they disperse. They will both catch and eat each other. If provided with plenty of food and a good deal of vegetation to perch on and to hide amongst, they can be kept together for a time without undue loss, but as they grow they will need to be separated. Their cages need to be tall enough to allow them room to fall out of their old skins when moulting. They must be provided with a suitable perch — a twig or a plant — as they cannot get a good grip on glass and would not be happy on the floor of the cage because they would be unable to moult there properly.

When the mantids are small, fruit flies make a basic diet, but it can be supplemented by gnats and greenfly if these are available. Later give them ordinary house and flesh flies and finally they will be able to take grasshoppers, locusts and crickets. They can be persuaded to take maggots by holding the latter in a pair of tweezers and waving them about near the mantid, and in due course they will get the idea and require less persuasion. Mantids go off their food before a moult.

Mantids do not have any particular need for fresh air and are happy in a jam jar with a screw top, provided it is large enough, but they are equally happy in a jar with a covering of netting held on with an elastic band.

Mantids acquire their wings when they are adult — as indeed do all other winged insects. After about a fortnight they will be ready to mate.

Mantids

Mantids have a bad reputation for eating their males. Unfortunately this reputation is often deserved. The best strategy is to feed the female all she can eat for two or three days and then introduce her into the male's cage. She may well permit him to mate and then start eating him, starting at the head which is, of course, nearest her mouth. This will not interfere with mating; indeed it is thought that the loss of his head will render the mating more vigorous and effective, though unfortunately he will not be able to mate with another female. However, one female may be able — if well fed — to produce a number of oothecae as the result of one mating.

The males and females are easily distinguished by looking at the underside of the abdomen. The females have six segments and the males eight.

Mantids are, as has already been stated, members of one family and their behaviour and life histories are all very similar. However, they differ in size — as adults — from just over a centimetre to about twelve centimetres and mimic all sorts of creatures and objects, black ants, leaves, flowers (even orchids), sticks and bark. Since they are often mimicking the same things, phasmids and mantids may be found which look remarkably alike. However, the heavy spines on the fore limbs will always enable one to recognise a mantid.

Mantids are preserved dry and need to be relaxed, set dried and finally pinned, though a specimen which has just been dried could probably be identified.

Sphodromantis is a common tropical genus. These are large mantids, 10-cm long, in the female and brown or light green in colour.

Phasmids or Stick Insects

There are about 2,000 species of stick insects, living mainly in the tropics, though some are to be found in the Mediterranean area, and two species of New Zealand stick insects have managed to establish themselves in the south-west of Britain.

The name 'phasmid' is derived from the same stem as 'phantom' and may refer to their often spectral appearance or to the excellence of the camouflage which enables them to disappear like ghosts among the foliage in their native haunts. In the United States they are known as 'walking sticks'.

They are large insects; the baobab stick insect, though very attenuated, is 30-cm in length, and even among the sticks that are popular pets *Acrophylla wulfingi* — the Queensland Titan — is 18-cm long. Such creatures have to be accommodated in a very tall cage to enable them to moult successfully. Stick insects are entirely vegetarian (that is if one excludes their habit of absent-mindedly eating each other's legs) and eat a great deal when they are growing, so you would be well advised to provide a very good supply of food plant, especially during the winter. Many of them take bramble in captivity. Most of them come from tropical rain forests and need warmth and humidity.

Their cages can be made from all sorts of materials, such as plastic cylinders with tops of netting, (in the author's collection some rather prickly stick insects live on bramble inside a cellophane cylinder misleadingly labelled 'The Best Soft Toy in the World' which originally contained a teddy-bear) or of netting supported on a framework of wood, cardboard or any other convenient material. Inside the cylinder should be a container with the food plant. A waterproof pot filled with wet sand holds the food plant in position and keeps it fresh. Stick insects moult by hanging themselves up and, as it were, falling out of their old skins. If they do not have room to do this, they will fail to moult properly and may die, lose limbs or end up distorted. They need a branch from which there is a clear fall of more than twice their length. Disturbance may cause them to lose their grip and fall to the floor, but all may not be lost. On one occasion the author rescued a partly moulted phasmid from the floor of the cage, pinned the already free part of the moulted skin (or exuvium) onto a bramble thorn and saw the moult successfully completed. Presumably the animal had not been struggling on the floor for too long.

The food plant should be sprayed every evening with water from a house-plant sprayer. Ordinary room temperatures are suitable for several stick insects, especially the older ones, but they will do best in the warmest part of the room, for example, near a radiator. Overcrowding will encourage them to eat each other's limbs. This is especially true of the Indian or laboratory stick *Carausius morosus*.

Food plants vary with the species but bramble is accepted by many species and privet and rhododendron are eaten by others. Bramble sprigs will often need cleaning up (especially in the winter), that is dead leaves and dead twigs should be removed. Before putting the twigs in water or wet sand cut off the dead end and split or hammer the stem to give a larger surface for absorbing water. With this treatment the food plant should remain fresh for at least a week or until it is all eaten.

A   Food plant container
B   Gauze panel

The droppings of phasmids are dry and inoffensive and provided that the bottom of the cage is dry and the cage is not overcrowded can be left for a few days. Several species drop their eggs to the ground, so if it is desired to hatch them the eggs will have to be separated out.

Most of the stick insects that are commonly kept are parthenogenetic — that is to say unfertilized eggs develop nearly always producing females. This solves the problem of determining the sex!

The eggs are mostly small dark seed-like objects with sculpturing which varies from genus to genus. It seems impossible that a phasmid 12-mm long can emerge from an egg of such small dimensions.

Many phasmids have a long incubation period; periods of up to nine months are quite normal and an incubation time of two years is not abnormal. The recommended practice is to keep the eggs on clean moist sand in a transparent plastic box. The nymphs will need to be moved onto the food plant as soon as they have recovered from hatching. The food plant should be sprayed with fine droplets of water as newly hatched nymphs need water. Small nymphs need a little more care than fully grown stick insects. The cage must be kept clean and free of mould. Mould is particularly likely to grow on damp droppings at the bottom of the cage. Nymphs can get trapped in free water, (whether it is condensed on the walls of the cage or in the pot containing the food plant) and drown. They are also, of course, more vulnerable to starvation and dehydration.

There are quite a lot of different species available in Britain and a few of the most popular are described here.

Carausius morosus, the Indian stick or laboratory stick, is the easiest to keep in captivity. Since its discovery in India at the beginning of the century it has become a very familiar pet in schools and homes and is now thoroughly domesticated. Though males turn up occasionally, mating has never been observed and it is to all intents and purposes entirely parthenogenetic. Adult females are about 75-mm in length and coloured in various shades of green or brown, usually with red at the base of the first pair of legs. They have no wings.

Unlike so many other stick insects it does not like bramble and it is usually fed on privet or ivy. They will also take a variety of other evergreen plants and can be a nuisance if they get established in a greenhouse.

It is not the most exciting of phasmids, being a nocturnal creature as indeed are many of the others. However, there are a number of interesting experiments demonstrating variation of colour with changes in temperature and humidity and light which can be tried on the Indian stick. When disturbed it plays dead, going into a state of reflex rigidity, thus demonstrating a form of defence which is fairly common among the arthropods.

Facing page:
A *Bacillus rossius* Female ×⅔
B *Extatosoma tiaratum* Nymph ×⅔
C *Sipyloidea sipylus* Nymph ×⅔
D *Phyllium bioculatum* Female ×½
E *Carausius morosus* Female ×⅔

Bacillus rossius, the Corsican stick insect, comes from Southern Europe. There is another similar species, *Bacillus gallicus* (sometimes known as *Clonopsis gallica)* from the same region. but it is now thought that most of the Corsican sticks in captivity belong to the species *Bacillus rossius.* Both species are parthenogenetic in captivity, males being rarely found, even in the wild. This species is wingless and the adult has a body length of about 65-mm. It may be coloured bright green. fawn or brown, with the base of the forelegs red. and there is sometimes a red line down the side of the body.

It feeds on brambles, rose or raspberry.

It is less nocturnal in its habits than some stick insects and feeds and even moults during daylight. Its eggs are allowed to fall to the ground.

Sipyloidea sipylus, the Pink Winged or Madagascan stick insect, is parthenogenetic. The species comes from Australia and males occur in the wild, but the stock which became naturalised in Madagascar appears to be parthenogenetic and the captive stock is presumably derived from the Madagascan sticks. The adult female is pink, though the nymphs are green, and she has short pink wings with which she will make brief flights usually in a downward direction. She is about 85-mm long with elegant long antennae. She is nocturnal and will not feed or willingly move except in the dark so, although rather ornamental, the Madagascan stick is not very exciting. Like the previous species they do well in ordinary room temperatures. Bramble is the standard food plant. Unlike most other stick insects they do not normally drop their eggs but glue them to the sides of the cage or food plant, both leaves and twigs. These hatch in as little as ten weeks into an unusually large nymph.

Extatosoma tiaratum, or Macleay's Spectre, comes from Australia and New Guinea. This striking phasmid has both sexes and the sexes are so different that they can be told apart at an early age. The adult male is fully winged and flies freely, even being able to fly upwards, unlike many stick insects. The adult female, a massive spiny animal 120-mm long and weighing 20-gm or more, has only tiny vestigial wings and cannot fly.

45

In captivity this species takes bramble and has been fed on oak. In the wild it feeds on *Eucalyptus sp.* It does best at a temperature of 24°C (75°F) or above in a humid atmosphere, but the older nymphs survive and grow in a centrally-heated room at ordinary temperatures with the food plant sprayed every evening.

One of the fascinating things about this species is the way it changes from a fast moving ant-like creature into a slowly moving one with the appearance of a prickly dried-up leaf. It assumes strange and impressive poses and can give a fierce kick with its hind legs.

Phyllium bioculatum, the Javanese Leaf Insect, is camouflaged to look like a leaf rather than a twig. It is included because of its unusual appearance, in spite of the fact that it is a difficult species to maintain. At all stages, including the egg, it requires warmth 24°C (75°F) at least and high humidity. These conditions are always difficult in captivity because they encourage mould, which in the wild is kept under some control by air movements. There are two sexes which are much alike though the male is smaller and slimmer than the female and fully winged. The adult female is above 70-mm long and has three-quarter length wings which, however, are not useful for flight. They eat bramble.

Anisomorpha buprestoides, the Florida stick, comes from the Southern United States. Its main claim to fame is its ability to project a defensive fluid backwards from glands situated at the front of the thorax. This fluid can cause temporary blindness so the species must never be brought near the face. Otherwise, it is a reasonably easy species to keep, requiring a temperature of about 21°C (70°F) and feeding on bramble, rose or Turkey Oak *(Quercus cerris).*

The adult female is about 60-mm long with long antennae and coloured brown with longitudinal stripes of a darker hue. The male is similar but about half her length. Both sexes are wingless.

There are a number of other species which are available in captivity. Phasmids are preserved dry. They need to be set and pinned and the larger ones may need to be dried artificially.

Books

Stick and Leaf Insects — J.T. Clark. Published 1974 (Barry Shurlock)
Rearing Stick Insects — AES Leaflet No. 30 from AES Publications Agent, 129 Franciscan Road, Tooting, London, SW17 8DZ, England.
Grasshoppers, Crickets and Cockroaches of the British Isles — David R. Ragge. Published 1965 (Warne). (For the naturalised species).

Locusts and other Orthoptera

There are about 10,000 species of Orthoptera in the world, of which we have about twenty-six native species in Britain and some introduced species and occasional visitors.

They are in the main vegetarian or omnivorous and some have a tendency to be cannibal, eating up dead members of their own species and even attacking and killing them.

Locusts are kept for research purposes, mainly with a view to controlling or preventing locust swarms. One result of this study is that there are established methods of rearing large numbers. They are used for feeding captive reptiles and amphibians, spiders, scorpions and mantids. They are also attractive and interesting creatures in their own right.

It is not necessary to have special locust cages for breeding locusts. However, for continuous culture, particularly of large numbers, when it is necessary to maintain high standards of cleanliness, special cages are very convenient. If it is not thought worthwhile to buy a special cage, an aquarium topped off with netting, held on by an elastic band, is adequate. In either case a 60 or 100-watt bulb in the top of the cage or just over it will be needed. Locusts need both heat and light for at least seven, and preferably twelve, hours a day. The lamp should be switched off at night. The lamp should also be switched off for half an hour before any operation which involves handling the locusts. A day-time temperature of 32°C (90°F) is recommended with a night time temperature of 28°C (82°F). However, they will survive and even grow, though more slowly, at lower temperatures. In order to aid moulting, the cage should be furnished with a few twigs (which should not be kept from one culture to the next) or some chicken wire (which can be thoroughly cleaned and re-used).

The hoppers or young locusts are much like their parents, though without wings, and moult a number of times, attaining substantial wingpads by the penultimate moult and finally becoming winged. They do not however mate for a week or so; it seems to take some time to achieve sexual maturity. In mating the male (which is smaller than the female) sits on the back of the female with the tips of their abdomens joined.

An acceptable food is fresh grass, which should be renewed daily. Not too much should be offered — ideally only so much as is eaten by

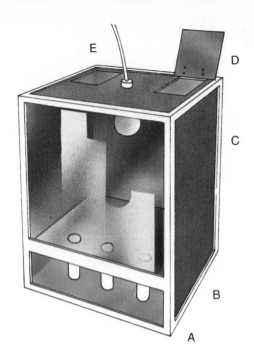

Locust Cage

A Oviposition pots
B False floor
C Light bulb
D Access door
E Gauze panel

evening. No water is needed, the grass supplying all the necessary moisture. Bran should also be supplied. If fresh grass is not available, an artificial diet can be made up with one part by volume of bran, one of dried milk, one of dried grass and one-tenth of a part of dried yeast. With this diet the locusts must be given water, which should be supplied in water-soaked cotton wool to the smaller hoppers which might drown in a dish of water. A bit of fresh grass added to this diet would help. In Britain fresh grass is available all the year round, even if one has to dig down through the snow for it. Alternatively, wheat seedlings can be germinated on moist cotton wool and kept in a warm place for about a week, after which they can be fed to the locusts.

To breed the locusts, provision must be made for them to lay their eggs in the soil. Tightly packed damp sand is the best medium and it should be at least 10-cm deep. Glass, plastic or metal containers are suitable. If the locusts are being kept in an aquarium, pots of sand can simply be put in the aquarium and a few twigs arranged to make a ladder. The females will find them all right. The pots should be changed frequently — every day or two — many egg pods laid too close will inhibit each other's development.

A waterproof covering could be placed on the pots and they should be kept in a warm place — ideally 28−32°C (82−90°F) — but temperatures down to 25°C (77°F) will merely extend the hatching time, which at the higher temperatures will be two or three weeks. The hoppers, when they emerge, should be kept separate from the older locusts or there will be a likelihood of cannibalism.

A recommended locust cage is shown. The false floor is of perforated zinc which, besides helping to keep the cage clean, allows room for the oviposition pots in which the females lay their eggs. A cage of about 50,000 cubic cm will hold up to five hundred day old hoppers or eighty adults.

Several species of locust are available, of which the most popular is the African Migratory locust *(Locusta migratoria)*. Fully mature females are dark brown, while the males are yellow with some brown. The hoppers are strikingly marked with black and bright orange if they have been reared in crowded conditions, but become progressively duller as the population gets thinner.

The Desert Locust *(Schistocerca gregaria)* is larger than *Locusta migratoria* and more delicate and susceptible to disease. It has a similar life cycle and should be treated similarly but with extra care given to cleanliness and gentle handling. The pots containing the eggs should be placed in the hopper rearing cages shortly before hatching to reduce possible damage.

The Red Locust *(Nomadacris septemfasciata)* and the Egyptian Grasshopper *(Anacridium aegyptium)* can also be kept in the same conditions, but the Egyptian grasshopper needs other green foods such as cabbage and lettuce as well as grass and bran.

All these creatures are susceptible to various diseases but the treatment of invertebrate diseases in general is beyond the scope of this book. *Locusta migratoria* is liable to pick up a nematode infection from grass that has been contaminated by other grasshoppers, so one thing that can be done if the locusts seem ill is to change the source of their grass.

Some people develop an allergy as a result of keeping locusts. The symptoms are rather like a head cold coupled with local irritation on the skin where there has been contact with the locusts. The obvious solution is to give up keeping locusts, which will solve the problem. There is an extremely useful pamphlet issued by the Anti-Locust Research Centre called *'Rearing and Breeding Locusts in the Laboratory'*.

Native grasshoppers can be kept in net-topped aquaria or large jars. They do not need additional heat, and will thrive if the floor of the cage is covered with slightly damp sand to a depth of about 2.5-cm. Fresh grass, changed daily, is a suitable food. Alternatively grass plants can be dug up and placed in the cage. They will still need to be changed, but not quite so often. Grasshoppers lay their egg pods either in the sand or in the grass provided. They enter a resting phase during which they must be kept at outdoor temperatures. This phase should finish by the end of December. After this the eggs can be brought in and half buried in the surface of very moist clean (preferably sterilized) sand. If they are kept warm — 25°C or 77°F is the recommended temperature — they should hatch in two or three weeks. They can be fed on grass and treated like adults. Care must be taken to see that the atmosphere is not allowed to get too dry when the nymphs are moulting.

The Field Cricket *(Gryllus campestris)* is very rare and is protected in some countries, including Britain. It is however more common in southern Europe where it is actually sold as a pet to those who enjoy its musical if rather monotonous chirping. It is reputed to make a good pet, thriving on moistened grass or lettuce. Females need about 2.5-cm of damp sand in which to lay eggs. The males engage in spectacular mock battles.

Gryllus campestris Female ×3

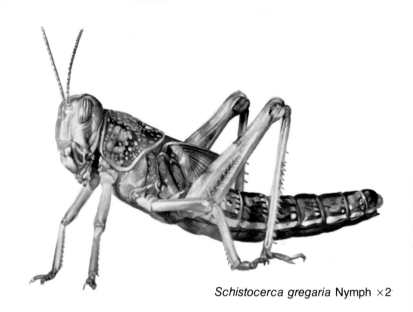

Schistocerca gregaria Nymph ×2

Locusta migratoria mating × 1½

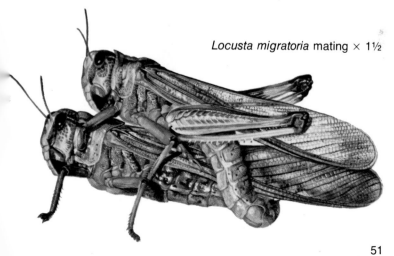

51

House crickets *(Acheta domesticus)* were introduced to this country some centuries ago and were familiar inhabitants of houses, singing cheerfully on the hearth. The adults are fully winged and fly freely, so would have to be kept in a covered cage. They are omnivorous and would probably do well on household scraps. Bread and lettuce have been recommended but the diet should be fairly dry, so probably bread and cabbage would be better. Fresh water should be provided by means of a wet pad of cotton wool. They will lay their eggs in this pad. They do, of course, make good food for large spiders and mantids. The only disadvantage to house crickets as a culture is that at ordinary house temperatures reproduction is rather slow, a generation taking about a year.

Other native orthoptera should make interesting pets. The Long Horned grasshoppers or bush crickets are omnivorous and sometimes carnivorous and should be kept in separate cages. Dr. Ragge's book describes and gives information on keeping all the British species.

Although cockroaches actually are more closely related to mantids than to orthoptera, mention might be made here of the Surinam cockroach *(Pycnoscelus surinamensis)*. No mention has been made of ordinary cockroaches either as pets or as a food species, because of the likelihood of their escaping and becoming a household pest. However, the Surinam cockroach needs greenhouse conditions to become established and so is a safer creature to keep, provided you have no greenhouse. They are omnivorous and would probably do well on household scraps. They need to be kept in a closed container with about 5-cm of damp peat or bulb fibre in the bottom. The warmer they are kept, the faster they will grow, but it would probably be best to keep the temperature below 30°C (86°F). The females are parthenogenetic (that is to say that eggs develop without being fertilized) and males are very rare.

Books

Grasshoppers, Crickets and Cockroaches of the British Isles — D.R. Ragge (Warne)
Rearing and Breeding Locusts in the Laboratory — P. Hunter-Jones (Obtainable from the Anti-Locust Research Centre, College House, Wrights Lane, London, W8, England)
The UFAW Handbook on the *Care and Management of Laboratory Animals* (Livingstone 1967)

Tarantulas and other Mygalomorph Spiders

Spiders, both the subjects of this chapter and those of the next, are all carnivorous and they are all predatory. With upwards of 30,000 species they must be one of the largest groups of predators among the invertebrates. The great variation in the methods of capturing their prey is what makes them, in the author's opinion at least, the most interesting creatures in this book.

The distinguishing characteristics of spiders is their use of silk. It is true that several other arthropods, for example, some mites, various small insects, and caterpillars, make and use silk; indeed in most people's minds the silkworm is the one and only producer of silk. Actually spider silk would probably be as useful as that produced by silkworms, but the latter are vegetarians and much better suited to becoming domestic animals than spiders. Spiders are the masters of the use of silk. Most spiders produce several kinds, which they use for wrapping their eggs, making cells to moult in, lining burrows, making trap doors laying drag lines, making bridging threads to walk along, ballooning, making webs, either catching webs or webs to signal the approach of prey or both, and finally silk to tie up and immobilize their prey. Of course, no one spider uses silk for all these purposes, but most use it in several different ways.

Spiders have ten limbs, eight legs and two palps. The latter are used rather like hands and in the adult male are also adapted for use in mating. Sperm is transferred from the abdomen to the palps which are then used to introduce sperm into the female reproductive parts. The male palpal organs are not always easy to see among the Mygalomorphs but are frequently very prominent in Araneamorph spiders. The Mygalomorph males of many species also have spurs on the tibia of either the first or the second pair of legs. If the latter are not present, a close look at the end of the palp should determine whether or not the male palpal organ is present.

The spiders are divided into two suborders, the Orthognatha or Mygalomorphs and the Labidognatha or Araneamorphs or 'true spiders', according to which way their fangs move.

As can be seen from the illustration, the Araneamorph's fangs move round an axis which is parallel to the body, but the Mygalomorph's fangs fold up underneath the body. This means that when the Mygalomorph is standing on the ground — as it often is — it must rear its cephalothorax (the front section of its body) up in order to free its fangs for attack. A rampant Mygalomorph can look extremely fierce though they have been known to fall over backwards, entirely spoiling the effect. Nevertheless, it is prudent in these circumstances to retreat. Even if the spider is known to be more or less non-poisonous, it is not pleasant to have a needle-sharp fang stuck into you and remember that any bite can introduce harmful bacteria into the system. A human bite, for example, can be serious.

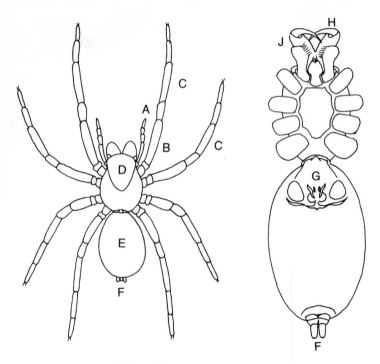

Spider Dorsal and Ventral View

A	Palp	F	Spinners
B	Leg	G	Epigyne (Female
C	Tibia		reproductive part)
D	Cephalothorax	H	Fang
E	Abdomen	J	Chelicera

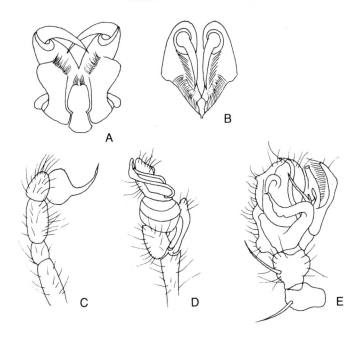

A Araneamorph chelicerae and Fangs
B Mygalomorph chelicerae and Fangs
C Palp of Male Mygalomorph spider
D Palp of Male Araneamorph spider, Simple type
E Palp of Male Araneamorph spider, Complicated type

The Mygalomorphs are divided into a number of families, of which the best known are the Theraphosidae, the family which numbers among its members the largest spiders. They are commonly known as tarantulas in America, or sometimes bird-eating spiders. In Africa they are called baboon or monkey spiders. The name tarantula originally belonged to the wolf spider (one of the Araneamorphs) found in Southern Europe which very vaguely resembles some of the Theraphosids found in the southern states of America. Early settlers (who were, presumably, not over-worried about taxonomic accuracy) transferred the name to the Theraphosids and it is the latter which will be described as tarantulas in this book.

Tarantulas are, compared with most of the creatures considered in this book, expensive pets and often hard to come by. There are fears that over-collecting could damage the wild stocks in some places and it is true that when the males go courting they are large and obvious and rather easily caught. So, perhaps, it would be wise for aspiring tarantula owners to begin by keeping some of the easy and readily available Araneamorph spiders, for example, the large common house spiders *(Tegenaria sp.)* described in the next chapter. This should help one to get the feel of spider keeping.

More than six hundred species of Theraphosidae (that is tarantulas) have been described and named and unfortunately they are not easy to identify and the taxonomic position is sometimes a bit confused. One of the most popular genera is *Eurypelma,* which is also known as *Aphonopelma.*

It is, however, much easier to decide whether or not a spider belongs to the Theraphosidae. As the picture shows, their legs are strong and they sit squarely on the ground on which many species live. Some burrow and some are arboreal, living in holes in trees usually surrounded by a mass of fine sheet web. These latter tend to have longer legs. Their feet, or tarsi, have thick pads of special hairs on the underside which are remarkably adhesive, enabling them to climb vertical glass walls provided they are given time to lay down a few silk threads to help. Young spiders can walk upside down on the plastic ceiling of their cage. They are sometimes described as 'brush-footed'. Tarantulas are large, as spiders go, with a body length of 50−90-mm and *Theraphosa leblondi* (the largest) has a leg span of 25-cm.

The abdomen of a spider is not well protected, having a thin and rather elastic skin. The result is that large spiders are apt to be killed by quite a small fall, the abdomen splitting on impact. This particularly applies to tarantulas but is also true of large Araneamorphs, such as some of the big Argiopids. Small spiders can fall slowly on a drag line but the tarantulas and some other big spiders do not manufacture a drag line strong enough to support them. So it is essential to make sure that a tarantula is not dropped (even a foot) or allowed to walk off the edge of a table.

Although most tarantulas are only mildly poisonous — which is to say that any symptoms following a bite should be mild and probably local, unless the victim has the misfortune to be hypersensitive — the urticating hairs can be a nuisance to anyone who is sensitive to them. These hairs are certainly used by the spiders to defend themselves and possibly they may also be used to subdue their prey. A bald patch is often noticeable on the back of the abdomen where the spider has rubbed it with her rear legs releasing clouds of fine hairs which are quite distressing, particularly

Eurypelma chalcodes Female ×²⁄₃

Eurypelma mesomelas Male ×²⁄₃

Eurypelma mesomelas
Female ×²⁄₃

Eurypelma smithii Female ×²⁄₃

if they get into the eyes or down the throat. At this point one should shut up the cage and leave to spider to recover her temper. Even if the spider never releases urticating hairs they come loose in the cage and get mixed with the web and other matter, so if one is sensitive it is necessary to be careful when cleaning the cage. Fortunately the cage does not really need to be cleaned more than once a year or so.

Cages for tarantulas do not need to be very large. As long as the spider has room to move about, stretch her legs and take a few steps she seems perfectly happy and healthy without a lot of exercise. The cage will need a strong lid, which is fastened down or weighted. Tarantulas are quite strong and all too good at escaping from captivity. They should have a little air but do not need a lot of ventilation. Birds and mammals have an excessive need for oxygen and, indeed, for food in order to maintain the high and constant temperature which is essential to them. One cannot judge a tarantula's needs by one's own. Peat, or for the desert species sand, may be used to floor the cage. Burrowing tarantulas will appreciate an old toilet roll centre in which, though it seems a tight fit, they will sit for hours or even days. Arboreal species will be made to feel at home by a good sized piece of bark placed in the cage. If stones or rocks are put in the cage, care must be taken to ensure that the rocks cannot move when the cage is picked up or they may roll on the spider and cause damage.

There is generally no need to handle tarantulas. They can, when necessary, be encouraged to walk from cage to cage but otherwise can be left alone. However, if the owner wishes to handle the spider, this must be done very gently. It is probably best to start by gently stroking the spider to see her reactions and then possibly by encouraging her to walk on to the bare hand. It is not a good idea to allow her to walk on one's clothes as the two tiny claws on each foot become entangled in the material and it is difficult to disentangle them without harming the spider. What is more, before the eighth foot has been extricated one of the remaining seven will become entangled again!

Tarantulas can sometimes be persuaded to accept small pieces of fresh raw meat but generally they need live food. For adults and the larger immatures, locusts and other grasshoppers make suitable food. They also take crickets, large woodlice, earthworms and large beetles. The spiderlings, or baby tarantulas, eat gentles or domestic flies and small locusts or crickets. Fruit flies are too small and difficult for them to get hold of. Tarantulas and, indeed, spiders in general do not need nearly as much food as people expect. As a rough rule, the young will eat a meal of about their own size once a week but, of course, they go off their food before a moult. They can, if need be, do with much less. If they are getting or taking no food, it is a good idea to offer them some drinking water. If the food is not eaten, it is best to remove it. Live prey in a small cage can fuss a spider who is old or about to moult. However, by watching your spider's reactions, you will soon realise when she is hungry and when she is not, and what her favourite foods are.

The excreta produced by spiders is a dry inoffensive chalky substance which is produced in small quantities. Consequently, the cage does not need frequent cleaning and an annual turnout is usually quite sufficient.

Tarantulas moult even after they are adult, usually once a year. While they are growing they moult much more frequently. When they are getting old, moults may become less frequent and rather erratic. Before a moult the spider ceases to eat and may give the impression of being slightly unwell. Tarantulas moult on their backs and should on no account be disturbed during this process. They may turn on their sides at intervals but should be left strictly alone till the moulting is over, which may take a day or so. Even then it is best not to disturb them until the new skin has hardened and its colour changed from pale grey back to its normal colouration.

Mating and breeding tarantulas present some problems but baby tarantulas are particularly charming and it is well worth the trouble. The first problem is to secure a male and female of the same species. It is not easy to identify tarantulas and dealers are not usually able to produce named specimens. For this reason among others it is probably best to start with one of the well-known species. Alternatively you could start with a pair of tarantulas but this is rather an expensive exercise and to start attempting to breed tarantulas before you are accustomed to handling them and caring for them does not seem at all sensible. The males do not live long and if you are fortunate enough to acquire a pair you would be advised to attempt a mating within a reasonable time. Mature males are apt to be rather bad tempered, which is not surprising if you consider that they are confined to a cage, whilst their instinct is to roam about searching for females.

Having secured your pair of tarantulas, feed the female well and place both cages together and remove the covers. The male will almost certainly enter the female's cage and attempt to mate with her. The two spiders rear up on their hind legs. The male will use his tibial hooks (if he has them) to catch the female's fangs which she has opened ready. He then stretches out his palp to apply to the epigyne on the underside of the female's abdomen. Mating is often brief, say five minutes, and the male will leave the female immediately after mating. With any luck the female will remain in the cage which has become home to her, but you will probably have to recapture the male, so it would be wise to stage these events in a warm room where there are not too many nooks and crannies for the male to disappear into. Generally speaking, tarantulas become mature and mate in late summer or autumn. The male will not be ready to mate directly after moulting, but growing restlessness will demonstrate his readiness.

The female will not lay eggs until the following spring or early summer and they will take two or three months to hatch, according to species. During this period the female will be nervous and aggressive and should be disturbed as little as possible. Humidity is important. In the wild the female is able to regulate the humidity by moving the egg sac from areas of unsuitable humidity and temperature to those where the conditions are right. For example, from the bottom of the burrow where it is cool and damp to the mouth of the burrow where the sun can warm the egg sac. If she is upset or unable to make the changes which she feels (presumably by instinct) to be necessary she is liable to devour the egg sac and the unhatched spiders. In view of this it has been suggested that it would be a good idea to take the egg sac away from the spider, keeping it in the sort of humidity which she seemed to favour and a temperature of about 24°C (75°F) and turning it gently several times a day to simulate the tarantula's maternal care. But, on the whole, it is probably best to trust the mother and try to present her with several choices of environment by, for example, heating one corner of the cage and supplying water in another corner.

When the spiderlings first hatch they are even more vulnerable. Exposure to light before their skin hardens and gets its colour will probably kill them. It is thought that this is owing to the effect of ultra violet rays. The young are best left with their mother for eight weeks, during which time she will not attack them, and then she should be moved to another cage.

There is a considerable initial mortality among the young, much of which seems to be owing to a sort of general feebleness exhibited by many of them, but there is also a certain amount of fratricide and cannibalism. This can be reduced by keeping them in a large cage and giving them plenty to eat. When the numbers are reduced the survivors should be caged separately. Alternatively, the largest and most successful of the spiderlings can be gradually removed and housed in individual cages. The young tarantulas must continue to be protected against the dehydration which is always a possibility when artificial heat is used and is a danger which one is apt to overlook. Their cages should be given an occasional spray (preferably with lime-free water, that is clean rain-water or cooled boiled water from the kettle) so that the peat is damp but not soggy.

Tarantulas are popular pets in the United States. Consequently the New World tarantulas have been more thoroughly investigated from this point of view than the Old World fauna. There is also some evidence that the New World tarantulas are more amenable to captivity than those from the rest of the world. It is only the New World Theraphosidae that are protected by having urticaceous hairs and it may be that their reliance on this form of protection makes them less nervous and less likely to have a serious bite.

Several popular pets come from the genus *Eurypelma.* This genus is liable to be known by alternative names which are placed in brackets.

Eurypelma (Aphonopelma) chalcodes. This spider, which comes from the south-western United States, is not strikingly coloured, being clad in shades of fawn and brown. When well fed she is of an amicable disposition, but it should perhaps be borne in mind that in the wild these spiders may get very little to eat and a year's starvation may make them aggressive, so newly acquired specimens should be treated with respect.

Eurypelma mesomelas. This species, which is also good tempered, comes from Costa Rica. It settles down well in captivity and has been successfully bred. The young mature in about three and a half to four years. The male will be ready to mate about a fortnight after his final moult. If the female is receptive there will be little, if any, courting and they will probably mate immediately. Each palp is used once, (one at a time) and the whole thing is over very quickly. The male and female must then be parted as they may well fight if compelled to stay together.

Eurypelma (Brachypelma) smithi. This very handsome and popular tarantula comes from Mexico and is sometimes called the Mexican Red Knee. Like the previous species it takes well to captivity and has been bred successfully. The remarks about the previous species also apply to the Mexican Red Knee. A further attraction of this species is that its striking markings make it readily identifiable and it is advertised by name in dealers' lists, so it is more likely that one could get a mate for a member of this species than for any other.

Dugesiella hentzi. This species is found in the south-western United States of Texas and Arizona and also in Kansas, Arkansas and Louisiana. It too is a popular species and is the principal subject of W.J. Baerg's book *'The Tarantula'.* Professor Baerg kept and bred this tarantula. It appears that his spiders matured in August, mated in October and laid eggs next June. which in mid-August produced spiderlings about 4-mm long. They took no food till the following spring. They liked termites which unfortunately (well fortunately really since termites are an awful nuisance) are not available in Britain. Small gentles would probably be reasonably easy for them to cope with. It took ten or more years for the females to become mature.

Avicularia avicularia. This species comes from Brazil, Guyana and Trinidad. It is an arboreal species and so has longer legs than the three previous species which are ground living. It is one of the most placid of

Facing page:
A *Poecolotheria fasciata* Female ×²/₃
B *Dugesiella hentzi* Female ×²/₃
C *Macrothele calpetana* Immature ×1
D *Avicularia avicularia* Female ×²/₃
E *Avicularia avicularia* Spiderling ×²/₃

---

the tree dwelling species, which tend to be a good deal more nervous than ground living tarantulas, and has been bred in captivity. The spiderlings are delightful with long translucent legs and jet black feet. The adults are dark with characteristic orange coloured toes. Their hairs are particularly urticaceous.

Poecolotheria fasciata. This tarantula comes from India and Sri Lanka and has been included because of her beautiful markings. She is arboreal in habit and her hairs, as she is an Old World spider, are not urticating. These two factors incline one to suppose that she will be highly nervous. This is indeed the case and she is no pet for a novice but should be kept only by thoroughly experienced owners.

There are many other species of tarantula, some of which may be available at pet shops and dealers. Another family of Mygalomorph spiders is the Dipluridae. Members of this family are characterised by the very long pair of spinners. They are, in general, smaller than tarantulas and lack the long silky hair. They live in silken tunnels under stones or in bushes and build sheet webs which can be very extensive. They are mentioned here *not* because they make good pets, but because some members of this family are dangerous. The dreaded funnel web spider *(Atrax robustus)* of Australia is a Diplurid and so is rather similar to *Macrothele calpetana* which lives in south-west Spain and is much feared there and in Gibraltar. Though not all members of this family are considered dangerous it would obviously be sensible for the inexperienced to avoid them. They spend most of their time hidden in opaque sheets of webbery and would not, anyway, make very interesting pets.

Another family of Mygalomorph spiders are the Ctenizidae or trap door spiders. They live in silk-lined burrows in the ground and finish the burrow off with a trap door which is usually so beautifully camouflaged as to be quite invisible. They are easy to keep, living happily in a pot of slightly damp sand in which a small house-plant is also growing (this helps to regulate the humidity of the sand), and feeding on fruit flies or domestic flies according to their size. Although simple, they are not exciting pets, remaining totally invisible unless one happens to see them reaching out from under their trap doors to catch flies.

Banana and other Araneamorph Spiders

The Araneamorph spiders are generally held to be the more highly developed branch of the spiders. They are divided into a large number of families which are characterised by their different methods of obtaining their food and caring for their offspring. There is a very great deal about their behaviour which is as yet unknown.

Banana spider is here taken as a general term for all spiders which arrive as unofficial immigrants — whether in bunches of bananas, other tropical fruits, crates of machinery, tropical aquatic plants, or whatever. A great variety of spiders have been recorded as arriving in this sort of way and in point of fact some Mygalomorphs are included among the banana spiders, but the great majority are Araneamorphs.

Anyone who is known to be interested in spiders will probably find themselves the recipient of a few banana spiders. The first step in providing them with a comfortable new home is to discover where they came from so that temperature and humidity may be chosen to suit them. This is not as easy as it sounds; for one thing a desert country may have some well watered spots, or vice-versa. Trial and error are all that one can rely on. A spider may demonstrate a need for more humidity by drinking every time a drop of water is offered to her. Except with very young spiders a drop of water can simply be placed beside the spider on the plastic wall or floor of the cage. For very young spiderlings it is best to offer wet cotton wool, as they may drown in a large drop. If the family to which the spiders belong can be recognised, then it should be possible to provide them with a cage in which they are able to spin their typical web or deploy their standard hunting technique. Spiders are all, of course, predatory and require living prey except in special circumstances, when they may take very recently killed food. Some banana spiders may prove to be gravid females and it is particularly interesting to try and rear the resulting offspring. If they already have egg sacs, they will probably be loathe to leave them and a certain amount can be deduced from the method of holding or fixing the egg sac, concerning which family they belong to.

Few spiders are dangerous, though nearly all are poisonous. They are not likely to bite a reasonably careful person and even if they do the bite may be little more than a pin prick. However, there are one or two types that are best avoided, especially by the beginner. The first of these, the

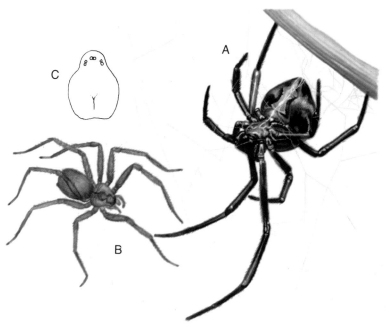

A *Latrodectus mactans* Female ×2
B *Loxosceles reclusa* Female ×1½
C Eyes of *Loxosceles reclusa*

Diplurids, have been mentioned in the previous chapter. The second of these is the notorious Black Widow, *Latrodectus mactans,* and other *Latrodectus* species. These are found all over the world in the tropics and the warmer parts of the temperate zones. They are not found in Britain. In France they are known as the Malmignatte, in South Africa as Button Spiders, in Australia as Red Backs and in New Zealand as Katipos. This spider is not likely to bite and it would probably not be fatal if it did, but the author has had a first-hand account from a victim and it sounded an experience to be avoided. Moreover, they are not particularly interesting spiders.

A third type of spider to be avoided is the genus *Loxosceles.* These spiders are light amber or greyish in colour. *L.reclusa* which lives in the United States has a characteristic violin-shaped mark on the carapace (and is sometimes known as the violin spider). *L.laeta* from South America is darker in colour. Both these spiders are known to live in houses and may give dangerous bites. Typically this happens when they have taken shelter in clothes. *L.rufescens* lives under stones in Southern

Europe. The members of this genus make a rough sheet of sticky silk in which they capture crawling insects and such like. They have only six eyes, which are arranged as shown in the diagram, and a characteristic way of sidling rapidly over the ground. Various species from this genus have become established in houses in temperate climes, and it would be foolish to risk such a possibility with this spider.

Spiders can be kept in small plastic boxes, lunch boxes and aquaria topped with net or, for small spiderlings, with muslin. Some benefit from having special cages made for them from shoe boxes and so on. Some like a small cardboard retreat in one corner.

They can be fed on fruit flies, gentles, house and flesh flies etc. Very small spiderlings can be difficult to feed. Cabbage or greenhouse white-flies *(Aleyrodes sp.),* greenfly, or aphids, small springtails, the larvae of fruit flies are all possible sources of food. Greenfly are easiest to handle when a family of spiderlings are being reared together in an aquarium and a sprig covered with greenfly can be put into the cage. Otherwise, they are difficult, sticky things to handle. Mosquitos are a popular food too and some spiders like woodlice. The author keeps a large plastic bowl in which to perform all operations which entail opening the cage of any spider. Then if the spider leaves the cage it can usually be recaptured as it climbs the side of the bowl. Probably it is good for them to have an occasional run around. Now to consider a few of the commoner and better known families.

Dysderidae is a rather primitive family containing both hunting and web-building species. *Dysdera crocata,* a native of Britain, is now found world wide. In Britain it lives both in houses and in the wild. It is happy in a comparatively small cage and will eat flies and woodlice and probably many other foods. Like most spiders it can climb up the sides of a glass or plastic cage and it is surprisingly quick on its feet.

Two other genera, *Segestria* and *Ariadna,* live a sedentary life in a tube built in a crack in the rock or a hole in the wall. From the collar of the tube threads radiate out across the wall. When one of these threads is touched the spider dashes out to investigate, and probably to capture, the intruder. *Segestria florentina* is a large dark spider, 2.5-cm long with iridescent dark green chelicerae. This spider tends to be found near ports and is, presumably, a banana spider which has become established in Britain. She is happy to eat the usual flies but her caging presents problems. Ideally she is installed in a horizontal tube which is arranged to open into the centre of the base of a box lying on its side which will provide the feeding area. In practice, if the tube is made of glass or plastic (covered with a glove of black paper) so that her activities can be watched at intervals, she is not very willing to take up residence and often builds her tube along one edge of the box. Alternatively, she can be

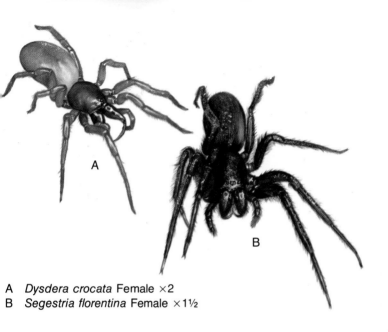

A   *Dysdera crocata* Female ×2
B   *Segestria florentina* Female ×1½

installed in a suitable hole in the garden wall. Once she is settled in she will probably stay put. Egg sacs are laid in the tube.

Pholcids or Daddy-long-legs spiders with small round or cylindrical bodies and very long thin legs are mostly found in warm countries, especially the tropics. *Pholcus phalangioides* is established in houses in Britain and is naturalised all over the world. These spiders build a rather scanty web going in all directions in the corners of rooms, usually near the ceiling. The best cage is a shoe box with a panel of cellophane let into the lid, the whole being stood on end and secured with an elastic band. They can be fed on domestic flies, being able with the help of their web and their long legs to tackle prey a good bit larger than themselves. They only need feeding about once a month and can fast much longer if need be. The female and male usually mate without much courting and the male is not attacked by the female. After the eggs are laid, they are held in the female's chelicerae for three weeks or so until they hatch. The young are easy to rear as they are able to cope with fruit flies. They do not need to be separated at once, but eventually it is easier to ensure that they all get fed if they have separate cages. These can be large tubes stood on their corks or inverted jam jars. As they will have webs at the top of the cage, they should be fed from below. Other pholcids can be kept in much the same way and are usually easy to rear.

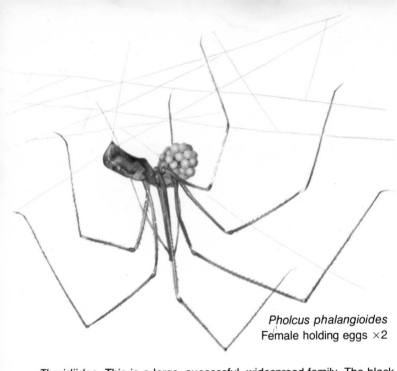

Pholcus phalangioides
Female holding eggs ×2

Theridiidae. This is a large, successful, widespread family. The black widow is a Theridiid, but there are many harmless spiders in this family and some are noted for their devoted care for their families. *Theridion sisyphium* is a common British spider on heaths and other rough ground. The spider builds a pyramidal web with threads in all directions and a covered retreat near the apex in which the green egg sac is placed. The young remain with her after hatching and are fed to begin with by regurgitation from her mouth and later on insects which she has caught for them. If a web can be found which is confined to one sprig of heather or thistle, this can be cut off and brought home, installed in a pot of damp sand (to support it and also to produce a little humidity for the spiders), and these fascinating processes watched. The spider will not desert her web. Theridiidae in general can be recognised by the typical body shape. They seem to take well to captivity, even in quarters that do not allow them to make the size of web they are accustomed to. *Steatoda bipunctata* is a British species that also lives in our houses. It makes a good pet and will live in a shoe box, eating flies and other insects, but it will also eat woodlice and ants, which are not accepted by all spiders. The female keeps the egg sac in her web, but the young disperse after hatching with no further ado. This spider is brown with a rather flatter shape than the

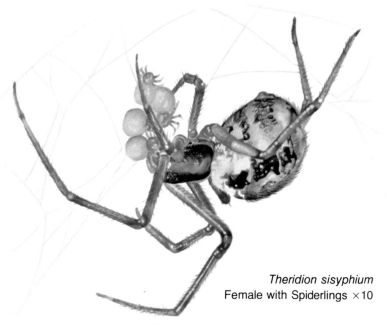

Theridion sisyphium
Female with Spiderlings ×10

previous species. *Teutana grossa* and *T.nobilis* are two large dark Theridiids which come to Britain, probably mainly on ships. They do like to have a retreat in their cage and do well in captivity.

Argiopidae. This is the family that makes the well known orb webs or wheel webs with a number of spokes and a spiral thread filling much of the space. These spiders are very successful and we have many species in Britain, including the well known garden spider. They are not likely to be found as banana spiders, though it is not unknown, and if they do, it is most likely to be an egg sac that arrives on some piece of machinery that has been out of doors (since these spiders lay their egg sacs low in the herbiage or under stones). The Argiopids do present some complications in captivity but they can be very fine handsome spiders and well worth a bit of trouble. The problem is the large size of the cage needed if they are to spin a proper orb web. It is possible to keep adult or part grown Argiopids in small cages since they are usually able to catch flies (of about their own size or a little smaller) in these restricted conditions without a web. Alternatively, they may accept food (flies or even gentles) handed to them (gently!) in a pair of forceps. They can be given an occasional drop of water or have their webs sprayed with a house-plant water mist sprayer.

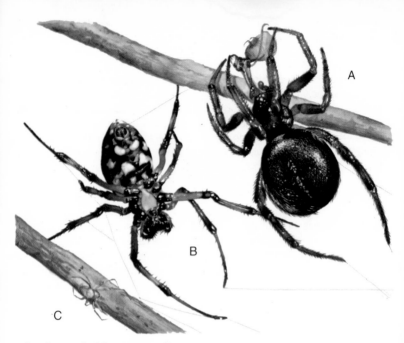

A   *Steatoda bipunctata* ×5
B   *Nephilengys cruentata* Female ×1½
C   *Nephilengys cruentata* Male ×1½

Nephilengys (Nephila) cruentata is common in tropical Africa and comparatively easy to rear in captivity. The egg sac should be placed in a large aquarium topped with muslin or very fine net (as the spiderlings are very small when just hatched) and a corked feeding hole inserted in the muslin. A few twigs in the cage will make sites for a number of webs. They will have to be fed, as soon as they have built webs, on small flying insects. Whiteflies *(Aleyrodes sp.)* are suitable and they will soon be able to move on to winged fruit flies. They can be left together (since little, if any, cannibalism takes place) until overcrowding makes a move desirable for some of them. A large number will die early on, apparently just being unfitted for life, and it will soon be found that some of the spiders are growing much faster than others. The males of this species are very small compared with their females. Adult males should appear quite soon, but females take a year or two to become adult. If they are released, they will probably build a web near the ceiling, and while they are adequately fed will stay put. On the other hand, this species when adult naturally builds a web which is much distorted with the retreat at the hub and only about half the normal orb web, and she is able to build quite a reasonable web in an aquarium. Other Argiopids can be reared in a similar way. Water should be supplied in drops on the muslin; the drops break up to make a fine spray in the cage. *N.cruentata* likes fairly dry conditions, but most other Argiopids like a more humid environment.

Agelenidae. This family includes the British house spider ('house spiders' in other countries often belong to quite different families) *Tegenaria gigantea* and the large house spider (only found in the south) *T.parietina.* These spiders do very well in captivity. They can be kept in a shallow cardboard box with a retreat in one corner and a cover of glass or plastic. They will build a sheet web which covers the floor of the box and will quickly notice and capture a fly or gentle or other large insect, such as an earwig or grub, which has been fed to them. It is interesting to note what good housekeepers they are. All rubbish and excreta will be found at the opposite end of the cage from the retreat. In ordinary circumstances they would throw it over the edge of the web. They can go without food for a long time (up to a year) and do not need water. As these spiders arouse such fear, perhaps it should be pointed out that they are very nervous, giving convulsive starts at sudden noises. Other Agelenids are reasonably easy to keep and rear, since their webs enable them to catch fruit flies even when they are quite small. But other Agelenids may need more humid conditions and should be kept in plastic boxes and given occasional drops of water. Their egg sacs will be laid in the retreat and the young disperse after hatching.

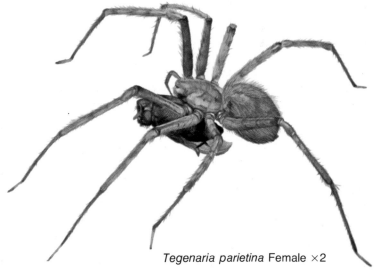

Tegenaria parietina Female ×2

Actosa perita ×4

Pisaura mirabilis Female
(Pisauridae) with egg sack ×1

Pisauridae. The Pisaurids are seldom found in banana shipments, but they are nevertheless a widespread family and there are two large, handsome representatives which are common to Britain plus one rarity. Although found roaming about in the wild, in captivity they usually establish themselves on one spot where they can be seen standing on a small web. Thus they do not need large cages in spite of their size, 1−2-cm in body length. Their courting habits are unusual; the male (of several species) presenting the female with a wrapped fly, so he must be provided with a fly with which to go courting. The female makes a round egg sac and carries it under her body slung between her spinners and her chelicerae. At this point she should be moved to an aquarium or other large cage as she will now want to make a nursery web about 10−15-cm high. In this she will place her egg sac and the young will hatch out and continue their development in its shelter. They do not need food at this stage. Then they will disperse and start an independent life. If confined in the same cage, they will hunt and eat each other, so they will need to be separated as soon as it is convenient. If the cage is large and there is a plentiful supply of food (fruit flies are suitable) the losses will not be excessive and it may be more convenient to leave them together for a while. They will need to be given a certain amount of water, a spray with the house-plant sprayer or water dripped on the muslin topping the aquarium, once or twice a week, depending on the species, should be sufficient.

Lycosidae. Some Lycosids or wolf spiders run on the ground and others make burrow from which they emerge, or sometimes simply reach out, to grab at passing prey. *Lycosa tarantula* is a large (up to 2.5-cm in body length) wolf spider found in Italy and Southern Europe and is the original tarantula. It is fierce and aggressive when cornered and probably has an unpleasant bite. There are other milder burrowing wolf spiders. The free running wolf spiders are not very easy to keep. They eat a lot for one thing and there seem to be humidity problems. The members of the genus *Arctosa* are the most satisfactory. They need 5–10-cm of sand, more or less damp according to conditions in their original habitat, to burrow in and will feed on fruit flies, woodlice and domestic flies. Their way of life prevents much cannibalism of the young, but it is probably best to separate them as soon as possible. Wolf spiders go in for elaborate courting rituals, waving their legs and palps at their females, usually (but not always!) receiving little or no response. The females carry their eggs attached to their spinners, which bump along the ground after them, and when the young hatch there is a period during which they ride on their mothers' backs. They do not feed until they have left her.

Gnaphosidae and *Clubionidae* are two families of hunting spiders. They build silken cells to moult in, unlike the spiders of families already discussed which moult out in the open, usually suspended from their webs. They also lay in cells and stay with their egg sacs until the young hatch. They can be kept in comparatively small cages and fed on the usual spider foods. They do not generally seem to eat woodlice. The author finds this group of spiders uninspiring and has never tried to rear any.

Ctenidae. The smaller members of this family. are rather like those of the previous pair of families, but the larger are often found as banana spiders, hailing from South and Central America. They are large (body length 32-mm) and some are dangerous.

Phoneutria fera has red chelicerae (which is considered to be a sign warning of a dangerous bite) and is aggressive in habit. These spiders should obviously be handled with great care. They do not carry their egg sacs in their chelicerae but tend to sit on guard with the egg sac attached to their spinners. They would probably accept flies and other large insects and would need to be kept warm.

Facing page:

A   *Misumena vatia* Female ×3
B   *Phoneutria fera* Female ×⅔
C   Heteropodid Male ×1 (found at London Airport)
D   *Drassodes lapidosus* Female *(Gnaphosidae)* ×3

Heteropodidae. Heteropoda venatoria is the typical banana spider. It has a body length of 25-mm and is found all over the tropics — presumably transported by men — and is much given to living in houses and other buildings. It is very popular with housewives because it eats so many cockroaches and other unpopular insects. This spider settles down well in captivity. It likes to live on a vertical surface and should be provided with a reasonably tall cage, such as a large jam jar. A solid roof (rather than netting) would be best as it tends to walk on the roof and also to build its enormous moulting cell near the ceiling. It is a hunting spider and makes extremely rapid darts after any prey which comes near enough. The long legs stretched out sideways and the characteristic movements have given them the name 'Giant Crab Spiders'. Spiders from the genus *Olios* also travel here as banana spiders. They require much the same conditions. In this family eggs are laid in a large cell in which they live with their mother until they are independent. She does not feed them, but is very protective.

Selenopidae. This is a family of spiders which look very like extremely flat members of the previous family and behave in a similar manner except that they do not build cells either for moulting or egg laying. They should receive similar treatment.

Thomisidae or Crab Spiders. The Thomisidae are not much given to becoming banana spiders, but the family is world wide and we have a number of very attractive species in Britain. Although these spiders do not make a web, they are capable of taking comparatively large prey. *Misumena vatia* can be seen in the summer, perched on a flower, eating insects a good deal larger than herself. They do well in captivity, being happy to eat large meals at rare intervals and live in quite small cages. The eggs are laid in an egg sac which is generally lenticular in shape and often fastened among the leaves of a plant. The spider sits on guard until the eggs hatch, about which time she usually dies. Although the male is smaller than the female, mating is usually conducted without much fuss.

Salticidae or Jumping Spiders. This family has long sight, lively manners, often beautiful colours, the endearing habit of looking round, and is a great favourite. They do not build webs but stalk their prey.

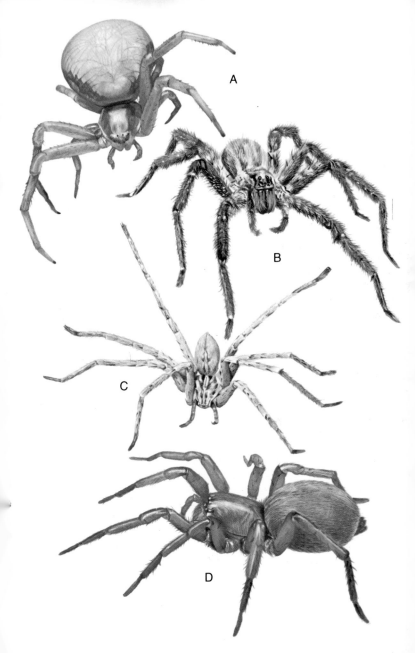

A

B

C

D

75

Facing page:

A *Uloborus walckenaerius* Female *(Uloboridae)* ×6
B *Stegodyphus lineatus* Female *(Eresidae)* ×3
C *Thyene sp.* Female *(Salticidae)* ×6
D *Amaurobius similis* Female ×2½

capturing it in a final leap. Unlike most spiders they have very good sight. They are not large spiders; 13-mm is a good size for a jumping spider, but they need comparatively large cages to give them room to hunt their prey. Their prey should not be larger than the spiders. They usually live in dryish places but they are often grateful for a drop of water. They need a good deal of room for courting. The male performs splendid mating dances, while the female keeps running away. It rarely seems to come to a successful conclusion. Sadly, the young are difficult to rear, as it is not easy to find suitable prey for the spiderlings, but partly grown spiders will often survive to become adult and will live for several years. There are particularly attractive Salticids in the United States. There are also a number of species in Britain but in the main this is a tropical family.

Eresidae. Eresids are found only in the Old World. None have been found in Britain for many years, but there are quite a few in Europe. They are web building spiders and from a special spinning plate called the cribellum they produce silk which is combed out by a comb on one of the last legs to give a fluffy silk which is remarkably adhesive. They are middle-sized spiders with body length 6–12-mm and often prettily marked. They do well in captivity, staying in their retreat most of the time, but venturing cautiously out to catch insects or woodlice that have become entangled in the web. They like a fairly dry atmosphere and warmth, since they come from hot places. They mate with little or no fuss and egg sacs are laid in the retreat. After hatching the young stay with their mother for quite a time and share her food. They can be reared at a surprisingly high density if supplied with plenty of food. Although there is no sign of cannibalism, even in populations of high density, the larger spiderlings tend to get most of the food and the others may, in consequence, starve.

Amaurobidae. These spiders are found all over the world, not, of course, the same species, but with more or less the same way of life. They also possess a cribellum and weave cribellate silk and build somewhat similar snares as the Eresids. Their favourite home is a hole in a wall and a bluish web can be seen on the brickwork round the hole. If the web is gently tickled with a grass stalk the spider emerges. They do

not like woodlice but will readily take flies. In captivity they seem to appreciate a retreat to live in and would probably be happy in most types of cage. They need an occasional drop of water.

Uloboridae. This family are not frequent banana spiders and the two British species are rare, but they are found more commonly on the Continent and in the United States. They build an orb web or part (only three sections) of an orb web. These spiders have no poison sacs and find it impossible to catch prey without a web, nor will they take food from forceps. They cannot build a web unless there are air movements to float the threads, so they must be housed in a cage which is constructed mainly from netting. Netting can either be wrapped round a framework made of wood or meccano, or panels can be cut from a cardboard box and netting sewn or glued over the apertures. Mosquitos or winged fruit flies make the best food, and the whole cage should be sprayed from the outside once or twice a week with a mist sprayer.

General advice on keeping spiders
If the abdomen of the spider looks shrivelled, it may be thirsty, it may be hungry, or it may be getting old. If it is getting old, its movements will be awkward and rheumaticky as well. If it refuses food and seems unwell, it may be about to moult. If it is continually lethargic, it is probably being kept at too cold a temperature. Generally speaking spiders do not need to be fed more than once a week, much less often for fully grown web building spiders, and a bit more often for very active hunting species spiderlings. It is best not to handle small spiders but to pick them up by persuading them to walk into a suitably sized tube. Dead spiders can be preserved in 70 per cent alcohol.

Books
A Guide to Spiders and their Kin — H.W. and L.R. Levi (Golden Press, New York. In Britain obtainable only from E.W. Classey Ltd., Park Road, Faringdon, Oxon. SN7 7DR.). This invaluable little paperback has a world wide coverage of spiders, also other arachnids, millipedes, centipedes and woodlice.
The World of Spiders — W.S. Bristowe (Collins, London). This deals only with British spiders.
American Spiders — W.J. Gertsch (D. Van Nostrand Co. Inc., Princeton, New Jersey, U.S.A.)
How to know the Spiders — B.J. Kaston (Wm.C. Brown, Co. Dubuque, Iowa, U.S.A.)

Scorpions and other Arachnids

Scorpions have a reputation of being extremely dangerous and a few scorpions are definitely poisonous, injecting by means of the sting in their tails a neurotoxin which affects the nerves and causes results which may be deadly and are at the least extremely unpleasant. *Buthus occitanus,* a large yellow scorpion found in Southern Europe and North Africa is such a scorpion, though curiously enough the North African specimens are said to be much more dangerous than the European. It grows to 5-cm in body plus tail length. *Androctonus australis,* the fat tailed scorpion of North Africa, is dangerous, as are *Leiurus quinquestriatus* from the Middle-East and *Centruroides* species from America. These are believed to be the most dangerous scorpions and they all belong to the family *Buthidae.* Scorpions belonging to other families are considered harmless, their sting comparing favourably with that of an insect. Scorpions with large, heavy claws are less likely to be dangerous than those with thin, elegant claws.

Scorpions are generally thought to live in very hot, dry deserts and indeed some do. However, quite a lot come from tropical rain forests and others live in Europe in places where the winters at least are cool. There is even a scorpion which is naturalised in one or two spots in Britain, and one species is found in Canada. Even in deserts many creatures are able to survive by finding areas of relative coolness and dampness. Small scorpions can be kept in lunch boxes, with a few small holes drilled in the lid for air. Larger ones can be kept in propagators or securely lidded aquaria. A layer of sand on the floor of the cage may make them more comfortable.

Fortunately the cages will not need a great deal of cleaning. If the scorpions have to be handled, a long (at least 25-cm in length) pair of metal forceps should be used and the scorpions should be picked up by the tail just below the sting. Scorpions are very agile and will turn round and try and walk up the forceps. If they can, they will catch fingers in their claws and they can give a nasty nip. Do not let go of the sting or you will get stung into the bargain! Alternatively, you can gently encourage them to move from cage to cage with a long stick, which can be dropped if necessary. Perform any manoeuvres in a large kitchen sink or the bath, where the scorpion cannot escape to a hiding place at all easily.

Scorpions can be fed on insects of all kinds — crickets, locusts, caterpillars, flies, and so on, according to size. They should not be overfed. Surprisingly enough they are likely to eat more than is good for them if they are given a chance. If they do not rush out enthusiastically for their food, but approach it in a lethargic fashion, and if there is half eaten food about and their abdomens exhibit bulges between the plates on the back, then they are being overfed. Overfeeding can kill them. Gravid females may have stout bulging abdomens and be perfectly healthy, but males and immatures should not be so stout. They should be fed about once a fortnight. They also need water — a pad of wet cotton wool from which they can drink should be provided once or twice a month.

It is not at all easy to differentiate between the sexes of scorpions. Males tend to be smaller, slimmer, with longer tails and longer, more slender claws, but sometimes have more robust claws. Details vary from species to species. The sex life of a scorpion is interesting. There is no copulation. The male approaches the female cautiously (scorpions are inclined both to kill and eat their own species) and catches her claws with his. Then he leads her about for a bit (probably looking for a suitable piece of ground) and deposits a spermatophore — a stalked package of spermatozoa — on the ground. Finally he leads the female over the spermatophore until she is in the right position to pick it up with the special organ on the underside of her abdomen. Plenty of room must be given to them for this process and they need a firm surface to receive the spermatophore. Scorpions produce living young. After birth they climb on their mother's back and stay there for two weeks or so without feeding. In due course they leave their mother and, scattering, take up an independent life. They will need to be separated shortly after this or there will be losses owing to cannibalism.

Euscorpius flavicaudis — the species naturalised in Britain — would be a good choice as a pet. It is not aggressive and would be happy in ordinary household temperatures. In the wild it lives under stones and bark and would probably appreciate a suitably shaped piece of bark or perhaps a potsherd to retreat under. It is only 4-cm in body plus tail length and is comparatively small for a scorpion.

Pandinus species are among the largest scorpions with body plus tail length of 17-cm. They look extremely impressive but are not dangerous. They come from Africa and should be kept warm. A temperature of 25°C (77°F) would probably suit them.

There are other interesting Arachnids to be found in tropical and near tropical parts, such as the Solifuges or Windscorpions. These attractive creatures, 1–5-cm in body length with enormous chelicerae, (or jaws) rarely survive in captivity.

The *Amblypygids* or tail-less whipscorpions have been described as making delightful pets. There are only about fifty species and they belong

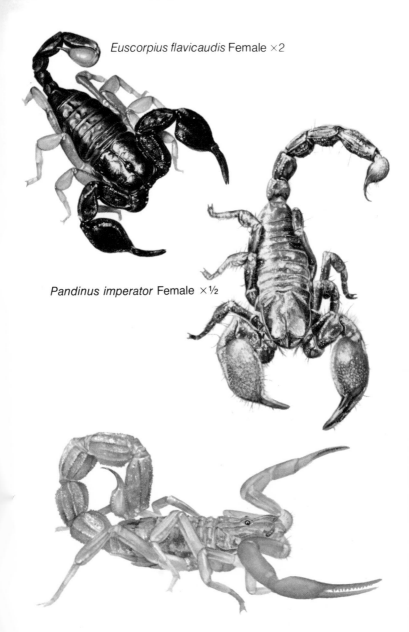

Euscorpius flavicaudis Female ×2

Pandinus imperator Female ×½

Buthus occitanus Immature ×1

to an ancient order which is presumably on its way to extinction. They probably ought not to be collected, but if one should come into your care it should be fed on insects and it would be worth offering slugs to see if they were acceptable. Water should be offered too. Since they like to hide by day, it would be a good idea to supply a piece of bark as a retreat. A large plastic box would make the most convenient cage.

The *Uropygids* or whipscorpions, like the Amblypygids, have no poison, and catch their prey by seizing it in their large armoured chelicerae. They too are rare and should not be collected in any numbers, if at all. They feed on woodlice, sometimes on flies, and have been known to eat small pieces of cold cooked fat. Both these species do not copulate and sperm is transferred to the female by means of a spermatophore during quite a complicated performance.

Opiliones or harvestmen or Daddy-long-legs spiders are never large. Even tropical species only reach 12-mm in body length. There are about 3,500 species in the world, including twenty-two in Britain. They are vulnerable to dehydration and should be kept in a suitably sized plastic box with a few air holes. Damp sand or damp paper towel on the floor would help to preserve a humid atmosphere. They eat a large variety of creatures, other harvestmen, aphids, snails, flies, springtails and so on. They hunt and kill these creatures but will also scavenge dead animals. In captivity they will accept bread and beef or mutton fat, but should also be given some of the small invertebrates already mentioned. They should be provided with drinking water. They mate without fuss in captivity. As it is difficult to sex them, a number can be kept together. They do not attack each other and the occasional cannibalism reported presumably only applies to already dead or dying animals. Eggs are laid in damp earth or sand, so if the cage is not floored with damp sand, a dish of it should be available.

Rearing harvestmen has been found to be difficult. It is suggested that this may be due to the unnatural constant humidity which results from keeping them in closed boxes. High humidity appears to be desirable when moulting, but afterwards a drier atmosphere is needed to harden off the new cuticle. Diurnal variation as the day warms up supplies this natural cycle of temperatures in the wild. Probably an aquarium topped with very fine muslin or netting would allow natural variation. A floor of damp sand would keep natural humidity available near it. The problem with sand is that it is difficult to see when it becomes dry, so regular attention is essential. Harvestmen are non-poisonous.

Pseudoscorpions or false scorpions are extremely small, 6-mm or less. There are about twenty-five species in Britain, mostly living in litter, although one lives in houses, mostly in bathrooms and lavatories. They are carnivorous, living on small insects. Although they are very

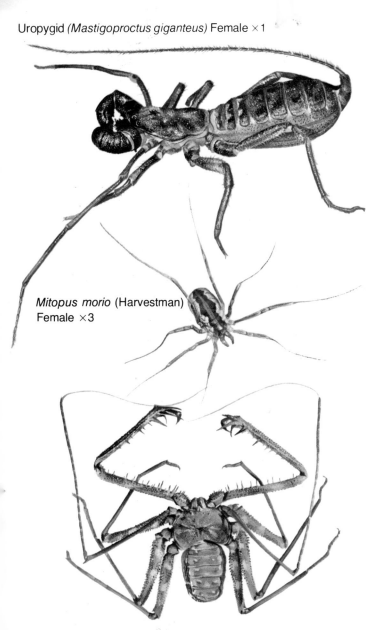

Uropygid *(Mastigoproctus giganteus)* Female ×1

Mitopus morio (Harvestman)
Female ×3

Amblypygid ×⅔

interesting, their small size makes them a subject for specialists. Arachnids can be preserved in 70 per cent alcohol.

Books

Spiders, Scorpions, Centipedes and Mites — J.L. Cloudsley-Thompson (Pergamon Press)

British Harvestmen — J.H.P. Sankey and T.H. Savory (Academic Press)

A Field Guide to the British Harvestmen — D.W. Mackie (From British Naturalists' Association, Warnford Road, Tilehurst, Reading, Berks.)

Millipedes and Centipedes

Millipedes and centipedes form two different classes of arthropods and the only excuse for considering them in the same chapter is that neither class has been over-studied and there is not much information about either.

There are about 8,000 species of millipedes known to science, of which about forty-four are British. They are creatures of soil and litter. The British species are all small, but tropical species belonging to the orders Spirostreptida and Spirobolida may be large, up to 28-cm long. It is not at all easy to distinguish between these orders, let alone to determine what species a millipede belongs to. However, some dealers import giant millipedes in large batches which are probably all of the same species, so it would be sensible to acquire a male and a female at the same time. Male millipedes have special organs for transferring sperm to the females. These organs, which are in fact modified legs, are termed gonopods. In the Spirostreptids and Spirobolids these are found on the seventh ring. They are hidden in a pouch so all that is needed is to see whether the seventh ring lacks legs. As nervous millipedes roll up at once, starting with the head, this is not at all easy. If they are placed in a clear plastic or glass container, they will unroll and start walking and by holding this up in the air, one may be able to see a gap in the legs. This indicates an adult male; otherwise the millipede is either female or immature. In mating, the two millipedes are wrapped round one another. Some millipedes secrete repellant fluids from a line of glands along the body. These are evil smelling and dye the fingers orange or brown. Some millipedes are able to squirt the fluid some distance, and it may get into the eyes and cause painful injuries.

Millipedes are mainly vegetarian, although they may do a bit of scavenging as well. They are best kept in a plastic box with a layer of oak or sycamore leaf litter. This should be kept damp, but not wet (that is, no free water should be visible). A small pot of fresh water should be available. The millipedes will probably eat the litter provided, but it is worth offering fresh apple or potato as well to see if they are liked.

Millipedes lay their eggs in the soil and may or may not enclose them in a nest according to species. Some species also build nests in which to moult.

Tropical millipedes need to be kept warm. A temperature of about 25°C

(77°F) should be suitable.

Centipedes are carnivorous and have a poisonous bite. They are generally fast moving and very flat and would be best kept in a closed plastic box with a few air holes and some bark or litter on the floor for them to hide under. They need fresh water. British centipedes are all fairly small, but the tropical *Scolopendras* can be 15-cm long. They give a painful but rarely fatal bite. Some dealers import these creatures, but it would not be sensible for a beginner to try to keep them. Centipedes are generally reckoned to be difficult to keep in captivity.

Both millipedes and centipedes are preserved in 70 per cent alcohol.

Books

Some information on millipedes and centipedes is to be found in *Spiders and their Kin* (see chapter on Spiders) and in *Spiders, Scorpions, Centipedes and Mites* (see chapter on Scorpions)

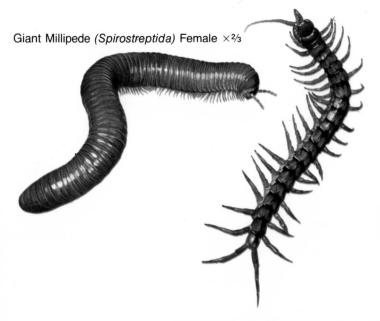

Giant Millipede *(Spirostreptida)* Female ×⅔

Giant Centipede *(Scolopendra Sp.)* ×⅔

Land Snails

Land snails and slugs are the terrestrial representatives of the Phylum Mollusca. This is a very large phylum with some 110.000 described species. In size they range from the 15-metre long giant squid, which is the largest of the invertebrates, down to minute species less than 1-mm in length. In the absence of a skeleton, a large terrestrial mollusc would, one imagines, have great difficulty in maintaining its shape. Certainly snails and slugs are all small creatures. They have no hard parts at all except for the shell (which in slugs has been reduced to a vestige, usually covered by the mantle or even been completely lost), the jaw and numerous teeth which are borne on the radula or tongue. These teeth are very efficient and the snail can often be heard rasping away at its food. Otherwise snails are silent creatures.

Snails, like all other invertebrates are 'cold blooded', that is to say they have no control over their temperature. If they become uncomfortably hot, they must try to move to a cooler place.

The diagram gives a much simplified idea of the snail's anatomy. *'The Young Specialist looks at Land and Freshwater Molluscs'* by Horst Janus gives a more complete picture of the surprisingly complicated anatomy of the snail.

The skin of the snail is well supplied with mucus-secreting glands. This mucus, besides deterring predators, keeps the skin moist, supple and clean. Glands just behind the mouth secrete the slime which paves the snail's path.

The body of the snail is ill-protected against dehydration, so unless the atmosphere is reasonably moist, the snail retreats into its shell, sealing up the entrance with a layer of insoluble mucus and waiting for conditions to improve. Snails can remain in this torpid state (called hibernation or aestivation according to circumstances) for weeks or even months and revive satisfactorily at the end of it, but they will then badly need a plentiful supply of fresh water. This is very convenient for those who must at times leave their pets to care for themselves. The snails must be placed in a dry box. This box should be of wood, since a plastic box may hold too much moisture for the snails to aestivate properly, and they may eat their way out of a cardboard box. They should then be stored in a place where they will not be subjected to extremes of temperature. They can then be left until their owner is able to return to feed and water them. Actually, anyone who has seen snails aestivating in countries in the south of Europe, perched on tree trunks, the stems of dead umbellifers,

Simplified Diagram of Snails Anatomy

A Mouth
B Eyes
C Respiratory opening
D Liver
E Anus
F Foot
G Common sexual opening
H Shell
J Stomach

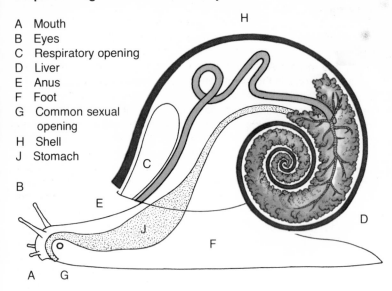

or even grass stalks, in the heat of the summer sun, will feel that there is no need to worry about extreme temperatures, but conditions in captivity are not necessarily equivalent to those in the wild. In the wild the snails choose for themselves suitable places to aestivate or hibernate and, in general, changes do not occur too suddenly. Slugs, of course, cannot protect themselves from drought in this way and must confine themselves to damp habitats.

The food taken by slugs and snails varies widely with the species. The giant land snail, *Achatina fulica,* eats a very wide range of vegetables and fruit, but some slugs and snails feed only or mainly on fungi, some scavenge animal or vegetable remains and some are carnivorous. eating worms, other slugs and snails or whatever they can catch. Snails need some source of calcium carbonate with which to manufacture the shells. A piece of natural chalk or limestone or, failing this, empty egg shells are suitable.

The problem of the determination of sex does not arise with land snails which are (like the earthworms which belong to the *Annelida,* a phylum related to the Mollusca) hermaphrodite. That is to say, they carry both male and female sexual organs but they require to be fertilized by another individual who will also, in general, be fertilized at the same time. This means that any two snails of the same species which are kept together should be able to produce offspring.

The giant East African land snail *(Achatina fulica)* is a popular and easily kept creature. From its original home in East Africa it has been spread, sometimes inadvertently and sometimes intentionally, to many areas of the tropics and sub-tropics and has frequently developed into a considerable pest. In East Africa giant snails of a number of species are eaten, and in East Asia they are fed to domestic animals, particularly ducks. Although it is thought that they would not be able to survive north of Latitude 30° (or south of Latitude $-30°$), care should be taken to prevent their escape from captivity in case they do survive and multiply. For this reason, it would probably be best not to keep them in a greenhouse, which might aid their acclimatization.

The average adult of this species has a shell about 10-cm long, brown in colour, streaked and mottled with purple, white and fawn. The largest known specimen was 30-cm long when fully extended and had a shell 20-cm in length. This species continues growing and enlarging the shell even after attaining sexual maturity. The oval-shaped eggs which are laid in batches of between 30−200 are about 5-mm long. They are usually laid in damp earth and hatch in ten days or so if they are kept at a temperature of 25°C (77°F). The first thing that they eat is their own shell and they will then take ordinary adult food. The young snails mature in anything from six to nine months, depending on temperature and food. They may live five or more years, especially if they spend some time aestivating. In the wild they are known to aestivate even though circumstances appear favourable for an active life.

They eat an impressive list of tropical plants and fruits, none of which they are likely to be offered by the author who also likes tropical fruit! Fortunately for them, they are happy to eat cabbage leaves — they prefer the outer leaves which are dark green — lettuce, carrots, dandelion leaves, potato peelings, root artichokes, apple cores, cabbage stalks and the stalks of marrows. It is worth offering them any non-poisonous green leaf except for grass, in which they seem disinterested.

They are best kept in a cage with a hard lid. This must be fastened down, as they are quite strong and could easily push off a lightly fastened lid. They are quite happy in rather restricted circumstances — say two of them in a propagator $20 \times 13 \times 16$-cm high with two small holes 6-mm in diameter. In this they can mate and produce numerous eggs. The eggs should be removed from the cage and kept in plastic boxes, otherwise the baby snails could escape through the air-holes and get lost. Also, although the eggs, even in these crowded circumstances, are not attacked or damaged by their parents, if they are left too long in their parents' cage, there must be some risk of accidental damage or fungal growth. Any eggs showing signs of fungal infection should be removed and destroyed.

Achatina fulica ×²⁄₃

In a more commodious cage the snails can look more impressive but would not necessarily be happier. The atmosphere should be kept fairly damp, which happens naturally if not too much ventilation is supplied. It is a good idea to have earth, leaf mould, absorbent paper, gravel, or something similar on the floor of the cage to control excessive moisture. Alternatively, a propagator seed-tray with holes can be fitted into one without holes. The floor of the cage then keeps reasonably dry. *Achatina fulica* being a tropical species does best at a temperature of about 25°C (77°F), though ordinary house temperatures should be satisfactory for them. The combination of heat and humidity produces a forcing house for bacteria and the snails produce a good deal of rather damp excreta, so it is necessary to clean the cage thoroughly about once a week. The easiest way to do this is to remove the snails, throw all the remaining contents of the cage away and refurnish it with flooring material, food and some source of calcium carbonate, and then replace the snails. It is therefore a good deal more convenient to have a plastic cage with very simple furnishings but, of course, more ornamental accommodation which is also satisfactory could be devised.

The snails look very fine, streaming along with their tentacles extended. If the animal is in a clear plastic or glass-sided cage, the foot can be seen from the underside. Dark bands move slowly up the foot as the muscular contractions drive the snail forward. Though, like all other snails, they have a tendency to be more active after dark, they are seen about by day, particularly if the atmosphere is damp. Fresh food placed in their cage will also often arouse them to investigate the food and start to eat it.

In common with all other snails they require a source of calcium carbonate. This can be a lump of natural chalk or limestone, a cuttlefish 'bone' or any other of the similar substances that are sold by dealers to assist birds in producing strong shells or — possibly the simplest and most readily available of all — ordinary egg shells. In the absence of calcium carbonate they will rasp away each other's, or even their own shells. They are also cannibal in that they will eat dead snails, but they do not attack the living.

Achatina fulica is the only foreign land snail (and generally the only land snail) readily available from dealers, but native snails and slugs make interesting and attractive pets.

The largest British land snail is *Helix pomatia* — the Roman snail, so called because it is believed to have been introduced by the Romans. This snail has unfortunately been over-collected in Britain and so it should not be taken, but left in peace. In the United States it has been introduced recently and is found naturalised in some places. It is perfectly proper to make a pet of it in these circumstances and should help to make up to the Americans for the unavailability of *Achatina fulica*. It takes much the same food as *Helix aspersa*.

Helix aspersa — the common snail — is a good sized snail with a shell up to 35-mm in diameter. It is easily found in the garden and, amongst other places, has been introduced to the United States, where it is also found in gardens. It will eat lettuce and other green vegetables, dandelion leaves and so on. The shell is variable in colour, usually fawn, mottled with dark brown, and the snail is greyish-green. Unfortunately it cannot be said to be one of our more glamorous species.

Cepaea hortensis — the white-lipped or garden snail — is very pretty. The shell is about 15-mm in diameter and is typically yellow, but sometimes pink or brown with up to five dark bands spiralling round the shell. The shell of the adult is finished off with a thickened white rim or lip. The snail itself is grey. They eat many wild plants and are particularly fond of stinging nettles *(Urtica dioica)*, on which they are often found roosting, ragwort *(Senecio jacobaea)*, also hogweed *(Heracleum sp.)* and other umbellifers. They like lettuce and other tender garden vegetables, and will finish off the tail end of a cucumber with enthusiasm.

A *Cepaea hortensis* ×1
B *Helix aspersa* ×1
C *Cepaea nemoralis* ×1
D *Helix pomatia* ×1

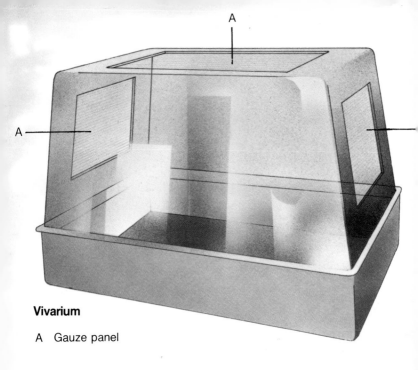

Vivarium

A   Gauze panel

Cepaea nemoralis — the brown-lipped or Grove snail — is equally attractive and easy to keep in captivity. It is slightly larger than the garden snail and has a brown lip, but is otherwise very similar and requires much the same conditions. Both snails are found in gardens, at the bottom of hedges and in such-like places.

As both these snails are small, they can be kept in a vivarium which is large by comparison with them. They are not powerful and, being native, they do not need artificial heat. All these factors make it practicable to set up a planted vivarium for them. Snails in general need damp surroundings, but they also need fresh air and most cannot tolerate stagnant conditions, so the vivarium should have a floor which is planted with herbs and some damp moss and walls which are made largely of wire mesh or perforated zinc. The cage should on no account be so damp that free water appears, whether as condensation on the walls or as pools of water on the floor. A propagator of the type which fits into a tray with holes which in turn fits into a water-tight tray would be very convenient. Large panels could be cut from two opposite sides and the roof and replaced with wire mesh. This should be kept in a light place, out of direct sunlight. Too much sun might cause the temperature in the propagator to become excessive.

The shell of a snail can be preserved dry, without any treatment. The whole snail — both body and shell — can be preserved in 70 per cent alcohol. If a snail is drowned in water that has been boiled to drive off all air and then cooled, the snail will die fully extended.

Books

British Snails — Arthur Erskine Ellis (OUP 1926; revised and reprinted 1969)

The Young Specialist looks at Land and Freshwater Molluscs — Horst Janus (English edition, Burke Publishin Co. Ltd. 1965)

How to know the Eastern Land Snails — Burch (Wm.C. Brown Co., Iowa, U.S.A. 1962)

A Field Guide to the Land Snails of Britain and North-West Europe— M. P. Kerney and R. A. P. Kerney (Collins: London 1979)

Index

Page numbers in italics refer to illustrations